Barbarian Rites

"Professor Hasenfratz presents both a solid introduction to the mysterious world of Germanic spirituality and something that goes well beyond the introductory as he demonstrates many deeper insights through his lively comparative and holistic approach."

STEPHEN E. FLOWERS, PH.D.,
DIRECTOR OF THE WOODHARROW INSTITUTE
AND AUTHOR OF *THE SECRET OF THE RUNES*

"A number of books describe the pagan gods of the ancient Norsemen, but very few explain why pagan beliefs appealed to so many for so long. In this outstanding English translation of *Barbarian Rites*, Hasenfratz engages Germanic spiritual tradition seriously and empathetically. He provides an important and useful resource for students of northern European religions at all levels."

STEPHEN HARRIS, ASSOCIATE PROFESSOR OF GERMAN
AND SCANDINAVIAN STUDIES AT THE
UNIVERSITY OF MASSACHUSETTS, AMHERST

BARBARIAN
Rites

THE SPIRITUAL WORLD
OF THE VIKINGS
AND THE GERMANIC TRIBES

HANS-PETER HASENFRATZ, PH.D.

TRANSLATED AND EDITED BY
MICHAEL MOYNIHAN

Inner Traditions
Rochester, Vermont • Toronto, Canada

Inner Traditions
One Park Street
Rochester, Vermont 05767
www.InnerTraditions.com

Text stock is SFI certified

Originally published in German under the title *Die religiöse Welt der Germanen:
Ritual, Magie, Kult, Mythus* by Verlag Herder GmbH, Hermann-Herder-Strasse
4, D-79104 Freiburg im Breisgau, Germany
First U.S. edition published in 2011 by Inner Traditions

Library of Congress Cataloging-in-Publication Data
Hasenfratz, Hans-Peter.
[Religiöse Welt der Germanen. English]
Barbarian rites : the spiritual world of the Vikings and the Germanic tribes /
Hans-Peter Hasenfratz ; translated and edited by Michael Moynihan. — 1st U.S.
ed.
     p. cm.
Includes bibliographical references (p.   ) and index.
ISBN 978-1-59477-421-8 (pbk.)
 1. Germanic peoples—Religion. 2. Civilization, Germanic. 3. Gods, Germanic.
I. Moynihan, Michael. II. Title.
BL860.H28 2011
293—dc23
                                                                2011018561

Printed and bound in the United States by Lake Book Manufacturing
The text stock is SFI certified. The Sustainable Forestry Initiative® program
promotes sustainable forest management.

10   9   8   7   6   5   4   3   2   1

Text design by Priscilla H. Baker
Text layout by Virginia Scott Bowman
This book was typeset in Garamond Premier Pro and Gill Sans with American
Uncial and Myriad Pro as display typefaces

Contents

Translator's Foreword

This volume is a translation of Hans-Peter Hasenfratz's study titled *Die religiöse Welt der Germanen: Ritual, Magie, Kult, Mythus* (The Religious World of the Germanic Peoples: Ritual, Magic, Cult, Myth). Since its original publication by Verlag Herder in 1992, the book has gone through numerous printings. In 2007 it was reissued as *Die Germanen: Ritual, Magie, Kult, Mythus* by Verlag HOHE.

Professor Hasenfratz's book fills an important niche in presenting a solid, streamlined introduction to ancient Germanic religious ideas and practices in their historical-cultural context. His text is well grounded in relevant scholarship, which he presents in a readily accessible manner. In contrast to any number of popular, neopagan, or overly subjective nonacademic books on Norse religion and the like, it is also thoroughly devoid of any romantic coloring. Hasenfratz is admirably cautious in dealing with the data that has been gained through the past few centuries of scholarship in archaic Germanic cultures. In this area there is much that is not known and will probably remain forever shrouded in mystery to some degree. Hasenfratz establishes from the outset how far apart contemporary Western civilization stands from these societies that existed one to two millennia ago. In his view, the best we might hope for is to be able to sketch a basic picture of older cultural ideas and practices and to gain an "approximation of the distance" that now lies between us and these very different older worlds.

In the past fifty years the most accomplished English-language scholarly monographs dealing with older Germanic religion and cult practices (such as E. O. G. Turville-Petre's *Myth and Religion of the North* and various books by Hilda Ellis Davidson[1]) have typically focused entirely on Viking Age Scandinavia. Though much of the material that Hasenfratz presents derives from medieval Scandinavian sources (which are often the most extensive and well preserved when it comes to pre-Christian Germanic myth and religion), he also frequently draws upon literary and historical sources from medieval Central Europe and Anglo-Saxon England to illustrate his points.

Barbarian Rites fills another rather unique niche in that it is written from the perspective of a scholar specializing in comparative religion and the history of religions. It is an interdisciplinary text that makes use of philology, historical linguistics, history, literature, mythology, anthropology, and occasionally folklore and archaeology. The text represents *cultural studies* in the best and most holistic sense of the term, and even seasoned scholars will undoubtedly find insights here that have not appeared elsewhere.

We should note a few things with regard to this English translation. In his original text Hasenfratz often points out etymological connections between older Germanic terms (preserved in the literary monuments of Gothic, Old High German, Middle High German, Old Norse, Old Saxon, and so on) and modern German. These elements of the book have been kept fully intact, but whenever possible I have also added—in the form of translator's notes (these notes appear in brackets and are labeled —*Trans.*)—similar etymological parallels to modern English. Because English is as much a Germanic language as modern German, these parallels generally serve to illuminate the linguistic material in a very similar way. I have added other notes to clarify key technical terms in the text, explain the historical-linguistic background of matters discussed, and to expand upon references that might be unfamiliar to the reader.

When discussing material that derives from literary sources (such as

Icelandic sagas or other medieval texts), Hasenfratz typically uses end notes to refer the reader to the relevant locations in German translations of these works.* This information is of limited use to an English-language reader who might seek, for example, to find out the larger context of an incident from a particular Icelandic saga that is mentioned. Because reliable modern English translations now exist for most of this material,† I have located parallel references in English for every such German reference, and I have included these in the notes ahead of the German citations. On the few occasions when there exists no parallel English translation, only the German citation appears. Perhaps some of these notes might inspire readers, especially students, to delve further into the cited translations of the original sources.

When Old Icelandic personal names are mentioned from the sagas and other sources, I have generally Anglicized these, as is now common in translations. Sigurðr is therefore rendered Sigurd, Starkaðr as Starkad, Þangbrandr as Thangbrand, and so on. A few uncommon coinages have

---

*In the case of the Icelandic sagas, Hasenfratz frequently makes reference to the German translations in the monumental twenty-four-volume *Thule,* edited by Felix Niedner and Gustav Neckel (Jena: Diederichs, 1911–1930). These translations are no longer particularly user-friendly, even for German readers: they are set in old-fashioned blackletter fonts and contain little in the way of notes and commentaries. Nevertheless, the *Thule* set contains much material that has yet to appear in more-modern editions.

†For example, besides the various modern translations of individual Icelandic sagas that have appeared in Penguin editions, there is also the excellent five-volume edition of all the family sagas: *The Complete Sagas of Icelanders* (Reykjavík: Leifur Eiríksson, 1997). A selection of major sagas and tales from this edition can be found in the single-volume compendium *The Sagas of Icelanders* (New York: Viking, 2001). In order to find parallel citations for many of Hasenfratz's references, I have also referred to various individual publications of particular sagas. The majority of them can be found in any major university library. A source for early Germanic religion that Hasenfratz frequently refers to is the ethnographic treatise *The Germania* by the Roman historian Cornelius Tacitus. Hasenfratz employs two German editions of this work. For purposes of convenience, I have cited the readily available translation by H. Mattingly for the corresponding English translations. For readers who would prefer to consult an edition with much more thorough and up-to-date scholarly commentary, the recent translation by J. B. Rives (New York: Oxford University Press, 1999) is exemplary in every respect. Neither of these English editions contains the original Latin text, however.

also been used, such as Ase for Old Icelandic *áss,* "god, member of the divine class of the Æsir," and Wane for Old Icelandic *vanr,* "member of the divine class of the Vanir." Another term that frequently turns up is Sib, used to describe the larger kingroup or clan of associated and interrelated families, which was a fundamental social structure in older Germanic cultures. More detailed explanations of such terms will be found in the text and notes.

In general I have kept intact the presentation and formatting of the original edition. When the author makes reference to specific words in older languages, and these terms are not proper nouns, they appear in italics and are typically glossed with their primary meaning in quotation marks. When older words appear with hyphenation, this is for the purpose of showing the etymological connections of their compound elements; in the original sources the words would have appeared in their natural compounded (unhyphenated) form. Words that appear with an asterisk before them are forms that are assumed to have existed during earlier, or proto, stages of the language (such as proto-Germanic or proto-Indo-European). These words are not attested in any written historical source, but they have been reconstructed to a reliable degree according to the science of comparative historical linguistics.[2]

Various colleagues and friends have provided their gracious assistance in one way or another for this translation project. These include Craig Davis (professor at Smith College), Joscelyn Godwin (professor at Colgate University), and Stephen Harris and Rex Wallace (both professors at the University of Massachusetts). Joshua Buckley deserves deep thanks for his careful reading of an early draft of the translation and his helpful feedback. At Inner Traditions, Jon Graham has been of inestimable support and Mindy Branstetter an exemplary and conscientious editor. This translation might never have come about, however, without the input of James E. Cathey, professor emeritus in Germanic philology at the University of Massachusetts. It was he who first pointed me in the direction of Hasenfratz's original book. This gesture inadvertently planted the seed that has now borne fruit, some years later, in the form of this translation. Along the way, he provided many kindnesses and keen remarks for which I am most grateful.

There are a number of German-language books that deal more comprehensively than *Barbarian Rites* with the known aspects of older Germanic religions. These include recent studies by Rudolf Simek and Bernhard Maier and the magisterial and still unsurpassed work by Jan De Vries titled *Altgermanische Religionsgeschichte* (A History of Old Germanic Religion).[3] Until these works are translated, however, their content will unfortunately remain inaccessible to English-language readers and all but the most advanced students. The concise and reliable presentation in Hans-Peter Hasenfratz's *Barbarian Rites* therefore provides a welcome survey of the fascinating and often mysterious world of ancient Germanic religions. May it find the wide audience it deserves and stimulate some of its readers to further studies of their own.

Michael Moynihan is a widely published author, editor, and translator. He holds a master's degree in German and Scandinavian Studies. His scholarly work is focused on comparative philology dealing with medieval Germanic languages and literatures, as well as the reception of medieval texts and ideas in the modern era.

His award-winning book *Lords of Chaos* (coauthored with Norwegian journalist Didrik Søderlind) has been published in six languages and is currently the basis for a feature film project. As a translator, he has worked on books and articles for both mainstream and academic publishers. He is a coeditor (with Joshua Buckley) of the book-format periodical *Tyr*, a journal dealing with mythology, philosophy, and cultural traditions. Together with his wife, Annabel, he runs a small independent publishing house, Dominion Press, which issues eclectic, limited-edition volumes in the fields of art, esoteric philosophy, and history.

Introduction

What Is Germanic?

It would be nice if we could discover some of our own history by studying Germanic religion—assuming that we ourselves are Germanic people or that we live in an area settled by Germanic peoples. It would be nicer still if by doing so we could recover some of our own identity—assuming that we feel our identity has been lost. In order to do this we first must know what Germanic means and who the Germanic peoples were. Were they the ethnic groups whom the authors of classical antiquity bestowed with the name Germani, and were all of these groups really Germanic peoples? Were the legendary Teutons, who harried the Romans tooth and nail, actually a Germanic group? The phonological form of their tribal name (Teutoni, Teutones) mentioned in the classical sources actually shows no specifically Germanic linguistic features and could well be Celtic (compare the Celtic term *teuto*, "people, tribe"). Were the bearers of the early Iron Age Jastorf culture in Lower Saxony Germanic? What about the early Bronze Age Jutish single-grave culture that preceded them? Should it be considered Germanic simply due to the fact that modern settlement archaeology or ethnographical research is incapable of demonstrating any breaks in cultural continuity for this cultural region up through to the Germania of the Imperial Roman period? If that is the case, then what are the typically Germanic features of this cultural continuity?[1]

If it is hard enough to say for sure who the Germanic peoples were, it is even more difficult to know what constitutes "Germanic" now. There have been those who thought that they knew what it meant, and their knowledge caused worldwide catastrophe. Were "genetic purity," "bravery," "love of freedom and honor," "straightforwardness and loyalty," and "stern morality" hallmarks of the "Germanic type," as is implied by the description of the Roman historian Tacitus (ca. 100 CE)? Is the Germanic world, therefore, as Hegel claimed, the fourth world epoch—following the Oriental, Greek, and Roman ages that preceded it—in which the World Spirit (*Weltgeist*) expresses itself most fully, the age of the highest level of historical human development as determined by the Germanic peoples? Or were honor and duty, as Alfred Rosenberg assumed, the "highest values" of the "Aryan (Indo-European) racial soul" most typically embodied in the Germanic race, so that dominion over "less worthy" peoples must in some way be an inherent entitlement of the Germanic human being?[2]

Although we may barely know who the Germanic peoples were—and those who thought they knew what the "Germanic essence" was may have failed in their claims of such knowledge—we can nevertheless be sure that we *can* define Germanic in terms of language, as the linguistic branch that differentiated itself from its earlier Indo-European predecessor through a specific set of phonological changes that are termed the Germanic sound shift. The Germanic peoples can therefore be defined as those who spoke a Germanic language. This language branch—and those who spoke it—are probably attested since the second century BCE with the so-called Negau helmet found in northern Slovenia. This bears the Germanic inscription HARIGASTITEIVA (which may mean "[dedicated] to the god Harigast" or "[dedicated] to the god Teiva by Harigast").*[3]

---

*Among the changes that took place in the course of the Germanic sound shift, the Indo-European consonants *k*, *gh*, and *d* shifted, respectively, to (*c*)*h*, *g*, and *t* in Germanic. These sounds can be seen in the Negau inscription in the forms ḫari-, ḡasti-, and ṭeiva.

What Is Germanic Religion?

We are now in a position to specify what we mean by Germanic religion. It comprised the religious practices of Germanic-language speakers before their Christianization (and continues after their Christianization to some degree in the form of folk beliefs). Although this external designation of Germanic religion may be relatively easy to formulate, what remains much more difficult is to describe what such religion consisted of internally. This is due to the nature of the sources. The most detailed textual sources relating to the religion of the Germanic peoples—the Elder and Younger *Eddas* and the sagas of Icelanders—were first compiled and written by Christians in the Christian era. These texts do not simply provide us with pre-Christian religious traditions; rather, they are the learned opinions of Christian antiquarians about Germanic religion, or, in many cases, they offer us a poetic glimpse into relationships from the Christian era (but not necessarily from heathen prehistory) in front of a "heathen backdrop."

Authentic pieces of Germanic evidence from late antiquity and the early medieval period present us with many problems concerning our understanding of Germanic religion. They often raise more questions than they answer, or they force us to rely on the aforementioned textual sources from the later (Christian) period in order to interpret their meaning. For example, someone who really wants to make sense of the Gothic runic inscription *gutaniowihailag* from Bucharest (Pietroassa) in the third century CE, or someone who expects to gain truly sensational revelations from this inscription with regard to Germanic religion may take their pick from the following scholarly interpretations: "[dedicated] to the god Jupiter (Donar/Thor) of the Goths, sacrosanct," "powerfully protected sacred object of the Gutania (tribal *Matronae* of the Goths?)," "ancestral property of the Goths, consecrated, holy," or "ancestral property of the Goths. I am holy!"

Further, what moderately informed person who assesses a Norwegian runic inscription from the fourth century CE that reads *lina laukaR* ("linen [and] leek") wouldn't immediately think of the relevant

Icelandic story—the historical value of which is highly debatable—from the Christian period (the thirteenth to fourteenth century) about an alleged heathen ritual involving linen and leek (and a horse phallus)?[4] It sounds even more daring when a Bronze Age Nordic rock carving of a god (?) with two hammers and a giant phallus is interpreted as identical to the Germanic god Thor, whose hammer is well known from the *Eddas*. This does not mean, however, that a prehistoric drawing depicting a god might not be able to help a scholar of religion to reconstruct the mythology of a later Germanic deity named Thor. A just as good or better source may be the Roman author Tacitus, who labeled Donar/Thor with the name Hercules (probably because of his clublike weapon) and who was otherwise knowledgeable in reporting all kinds of things about the religion of the Germanic peoples. But even Tacitus was actually concerned less with the German peoples per se than with his own Roman contemporaries. With his ethnography *The Germania,* Tacitus used the image of the Germanic barbarians as a mirror to show his own countrymen how Rome once was and how it could be once more: true to itself, brave, free, and chaste.

The term *Germanic religion* becomes even more complicated when we realize we must consider many Germanic religions. There is the religion of those who spoke North Germanic languages, for which we have the most detailed, coherent group of written sources; there is the religion of those who spoke South Germanic (that is, West Germanic) languages, for which the sources are generally more sparse and more disparate; and there is the religion of those who spoke East Germanic languages, about which we factually know nothing. Even within these respective religions there are specific distinctions relating to social class that we must also take into account. The religion of the court poets (for example, the skalds at the courts of Norwegian chieftains) may not automatically correspond to that of the bands of youthful raiders (Vikings) or correspond at all to the religion of the peasants or town dwellers—even if we accept that there was a certain amount of social mobility between classes. It's quite clear after all that a religion connected to a linguistic community and a particular class will change over time, and it is therefore also impossible to speak absolutely about a single religion in chronological terms.

Keeping all of this in mind, we can state what a description of Germanic religion is capable of doing. Only in the rarest instances is it possible to show how Germanic religion really was. More often, we can simply show how different sources portray it and how the Christian authors of these sources saw it in their own time. If these attempts at an approximation are capable of illustrating the distance that separates us from any "Germanic essence," they would in fact reveal a bit of the course of our history and a common property that allows us to become aware of our identity.

An initial approximation of this distance is afforded by the report of an Oriental traveler about his encounter with the Germanic people in the Volga region. It will serve as a point of departure for further approximation attempts. The report was written from a considerable cultural distance (the author was a Muslim), but it is not tendentious in that respect, because a depiction of the manners and customs of the Germanic peoples was not the actual goal of the journey he describes.

How a Muslim Viewed and Experienced a Group of Germanic People

Ibn Faḍlān's Diplomatic Journey and Travel Report (risāla)[5]
In the year 1923, Ahmed Zeki Validi Togan,[6] a Turkish scholar in Mašhad (in the northeastern corner of Iran, close to the borders of Afghanistan and Turkmenistan), discovered a manuscript dating from the eleventh century. It contained the complete report of the journey of an Arabic diplomatic mission in the Volga, authored by the mission's secretary, Aḥmad Ibn Faḍlān. Excerpts from the travel report that appeared in the encyclopedia of an Arabic geographer were already known to the scholarly world, and Jacob Grimm was aware of them. The Persian geographer Amīn Rāzī provides interesting variants and additions, probably stemming from even older sources, to the report in the Mašhad manuscript.

How did the journey come about? On April 2 in the year 921 the caliph from Baghdad sent a diplomatic mission to the Bulgars, a Turkic people on the Middle Volga. The reason for the mission: the Islamic expansion to the north had begun to falter. A Turkic people called the Khazars had adopted the Jewish faith,* and because they had settled on the Lower Volga, this presented a barrier to the political and religious advance of Islam in western Asia. The mission to the Bulgars, the northerly neighbors of the Khazars who were already partly won over to Islam, thus had the aim of breaking the Khazar blockade.

The travel route of the mission proceeded—while bypassing the Khazar territory—first between the Aral and the Caspian Seas, then in a large arc to the east, and finally south from Kazan to the Volga, or more specifically to the location of the Bulgars, the later capital of the Volga Bulgars. It was there that the mission came across the Rūs (Rūsīya),† a group of Germanic Varangians (Vikings). We are interested only in the section of the travel report in which Ibn Faḍlān describes the lifestyle and customs of these people.[7]

Text‡

§80: He [Aḥmad Ibn Faḍlān] said: I have seen the Rūs as they came on their merchant journeys and encamped by the Atil [the Volga]. I have never seen more perfect physical specimens, tall as date palms,

---

*The Eastern European Jews are more likely descended from the Khazars than from Semites!

†Compare Rossiya, the Russian name for Russia.

‡[The English text here generally follows the translation by H. M. Smyser, "Ibn Faḍlān's Account of the Rūs" (see bibliography for full citation). In Hasenfratz's original volume, the modern German translation of Faḍlān's text is based on Smyser as well as the German edition that appears in Heinz-Joachim Graf's collection *Orientalische Berichte des Mittelalters über die Germanen* (see bibliography). Parenthetical clarifications and bracketed remarks are mostly from Hasenfratz, although occasionally from Smyser. Arabic transcriptions have, for the most part, not been included. In certain instances, I have made slight changes to the punctuation, word order, and wording of Smyser's text to improve its readability and to bring it into closer accord with Hasenfratz's excerpts; any significant omissions are indicated with ellipses. —*Trans.*]

blond and ruddy . . . the men wear a garment which covers one side of the body and leaves a hand free [the right battle-arm].

§81: Each man has an axe, a sword, and a knife and keeps each by him at all times. The swords are broad and grooved. . . . Every man is tattooed from finger nails to neck. . . .

§82: Each woman wears on either breast a box [a shell-clasp brooch] of iron, silver, copper, or gold; the value of the box indicates the wealth of the husband. Each box has a ring from which hangs a [small] knife. The women wear neck rings of gold and silver, one for each 10,000 *dirhems* [an Arabic unit of currency], which her husband is worth; some women have many. Their most prized ornaments are green glass beads (corals) of clay, which . . . they string as necklaces for their women.

Commentary on §82: In Old Icelandic poetry, jewelry plays a prominent role in the kennings (poetic circumlocutions) for *woman:* she is referred to as a Wearer of Jewels, Tree of Gold, Goddess of Rings, Goddess of the Gem, and the like. Glass beads serve not only for adornment and as a form of money but also have an apotropaic function (as a magical deterrent against evil and misfortune). They are a common archaeological find in Nordic female graves.

§83: [The Rūs] are the filthiest of God's creatures. They have no modesty in defecation or urination, nor do they wash after pollution from orgasm, nor do they wash their hands after eating. They are thus like wild asses. When they have come from their land and anchored on, or tied up at the shore of, the Atil [Volga], which is a great river, they build big houses of wood on the shore, each holding ten to twenty persons, more or less. Each man has a couch on which he sits. With them are pretty slave girls destined for sale to merchants; a man will have sexual intercourse with his slave girl while his companion looks on. Sometimes whole groups will come together in this fashion, each in the presence of the others. A merchant who arrives to buy a slave girl from them may have to wait and look on while a Rūs completes the act of intercourse with a slave girl.

§84: Every day they must wash their faces and heads and this they do in the dirtiest and filthiest fashion possible: to wit, every morning a girl servant brings a great basin of water; she offers this to her master and he washes his hands and face and his hair—he washes it and combs it out with a comb in the water; then he blows his nose and spits into the basin. When he has finished, the servant carries the basin to the next person, who does likewise. She carries the basin thus to all the household in turn, and each blows his nose, spits, and washes his face and hair in it.

Commentary on §83 and §84: The reporter, who as a Muslim is bound to ritualistic prescriptions for cleanliness, reveals himself as especially sensitive to differing modes of behavior.

Regarding §83: From where did the Rūs obtain the female slaves whom they offer for sale? In the manner of Vikings, they attacked settlements, plundered, and committed improprieties. What they looted but didn't need for themselves, they sold. They engaged in predatory commerce; they were armed predatory traders. The twelfth- or thirteenth-century Persian poet Nizāmī reports in poetic form how the Rūs (the Varangians, or Vikings) came to possess slave women on their predatory advances into the Caucasus. It makes for a shocking account.

> They raged with fury, and as welcome booty
> They tore our women from their bridal beds.
> They robbed everything; not a single thing,
> Not even a toothpick, did they leave behind. . . .
> Of all the young girls, who blossomed here,
> They overlooked not a single one. . . .

In the Varangian stirs no sense of chivalry, for he only
wears the mask of a human;
A wild ass decked out in full jewelry,
They remain wild asses under alien hides.[8]

The comparison to wild asses is interesting in light of the words of our travel report.

§85: When the ships come to this mooring place [the trading place on the Atil], everybody goes ashore with bread, meat, onions, milk and *nabīd* [an intoxicating drink, perhaps beer], and betakes himself to a long upright piece of wood that has a face like a man's and is surrounded by little figures [idols], behind which are long stakes in the ground. The Rūs prostrates himself before the big carving and says, "O my Lord, I have come from a far land and have with me such and such a number of girls and such and such a number of sables," and he proceeds to enumerate all his other wares. Then he says, "I have brought you all these gifts," and lays down what he has brought with him, and continues, "I wish that you would send me a merchant with many dinars and *dirhems,* who will buy from me whatever I wish and will not dispute anything I say." Then he goes away. If he has difficulty selling his wares and his stay is prolonged, he will return with a gift a second or third time. If he has still further difficulty, he will bring a gift to all of the little idols and ask their intercession, saying, "These are the wives of our Lord and his daughters and sons." And he addresses each idol in turn, asking intercession and praying humbly. Often the selling goes more easily, and after selling out he says, "My Lord has satisfied my desires; I must repay him," and he takes a certain number of sheep or cattle and slaughters them, gives part of the meat as alms, brings the rest and deposits it before the great idol and the little idols around it, and suspends the heads of the cattle or sheep on the stakes. In the night, dogs come and eat everything, but the Rūs who has made the offering says, "Truly, my Lord is content with me and has consumed the present I brought him."

Commentary on §85: The wooden objects described relate to noniconic or nonfigurative divine symbols (so-called *shintai* images*). These are therefore not actual, figurative representations of a divinity, but rather "pole gods," like those that have been found at the German archaeological sites at Eutin in Schleswig and Oberdorla in Thuringia. At these sites there is also archaeological evidence for the ritual affixing of the skulls of sacrificial animals on cultic poles.[9] Such noniconic pole gods are probably what is also meant by the "wooden men," or *trémaðr*, mentioned in the *Edda*.[10]

§86: An ill person is put in a tent apart with some bread and water and people do not come to speak with him; they do not come even to see him every day, especially if he is a poor man or a slave. If he recovers, he returns to them, and if he dies, they cremate him. If he is a slave, he is left to be eaten by dogs and birds of prey. If the Rūs catch a thief or robber, they hang him on a tall tree and leave him hanging until his body falls to pieces.

Commentary on §86: The custom of isolating the sick person from the community and leaving him or her alone is found elsewhere (for instance in Africa among the Igbo). To my knowledge this is the only instance in which it is documented among the Germanic peoples. The manner of treating the infirm, elderly, and slaves is corroborated by other Germanic sources, which lends credibility to the report. Hanging is a typically Germanic death penalty.

§87: I heard that at the deaths of their chief personages, [the Rūs] did many things, of which the least was cremation, and I was inter-

---

*[The term *shintai*, which means "god body," is used in traditional Japanese Shinto religion to refer to objects, either natural or man-made, that are believed to contain the presence of a deity. Hasenfratz uses it here in a comparative religious sense. —*Trans.*]

ested to learn more. At last, I was told of the death of one their outstanding men: they placed him in a grave and put a roof [of wood and earth] over it for ten days while they cut and sewed garments for him.

If the deceased is a poor man they make a little boat, which they lay him in and burn. If he is rich, they collect his goods and divide them into three parts, one for his family, another to pay for his clothing, and a third for making *nabīd,* which they drink until the day when his female slave will kill herself and be burned with her master. They stupefy themselves by drinking this *nabīd* night and day; sometimes one of them dies cup in hand. When a great personage dies, the people of his family ask his young women and men slaves, "Who among you will die with him?" One answers: "I." Once he or she has answered, [dying] is obligatory; there is no backing out of it. Usually it is the girl slaves who do this [volunteer].

Commentary on §87: Seafaring peoples in particular recognized a realm of the dead that lies within the ocean or somewhere beyond it. For their final voyage, the deceased were outfitted with a ship, their most important and valuable cultural object. The custom of ship burial was also retained when the dwelling place of the seafarers was no longer on the coasts or when the deceased were cremated—they were then immolated together with their boat. Ship burials are documented among the Germanic peoples both from archaeological evidence as well as in the literature. A literary document from the West Germanic area, the *Beowulf* epic (in a manuscript dating from the year 1000, although the poem is older), begins with the depiction of this rite.

> *His own [the king's] dear comrades carried his body*
> *to the sea's current, as he himself had ordered,*
> *great Scylding lord, when he still gave commands;*
> *the nation's dear leader had ruled a long time.*

There at the harbor stood the ring-carved prow,
the noble's vessel, icy, sea-ready.
They laid down the king they had dearly loved,
their tall ring-giver, in the center of the ship,
the mighty by the mast. Great treasure was there,
bright gold and silver, gems from far lands.
I have not heard of a ship so decked
with better war-dress, weapons of battle,
swords and mail shirts; on his breast there lay
heaps of jewels that were to drift away,
brilliant, with him, far on the power of the flood. . . .
High over his head his men also set
his standard, gold-flagged, then let the waves lap,
gave him to the sea with grieving hearts,
mourned deep in mind. Men cannot say,
wise men in the hall nor warriors in the field,
not truly, who received that cargo.[11]

Concerning the so-called *Totenfolge* funerary rite (the "following into death," when living people are sacrificed to join the deceased; compare the Hindu rite of *suttee*), the northern Germanic area provides a wealth of substantiating material regarding those who give up their lives voluntarily or by force upon the death of another individual. There seems to be evidence for this in connection to a ship burial in the case of the so-called Oseberg ship.*[12] The excessive enjoyment of an intoxicating beverage (beer), often in tandem with the funerary rite, can be seen here as a solidarity ritual: it puts those who remain among the living into a kind of transcendent, paranormal state. This is the same state in which the deceased himself now seems to exist, whereby the funerary rite can be accepted as a "following into death."

---

*The Oseberg ship can be seen today in the Viking Ship Museum at Bygdøy, just outside of Oslo.

§88: When the man of whom I have spoken died, his girl slaves were asked, "Who will die with him?" One answered, "I." She was then put in the care of two young women, who watched over her and accompanied her everywhere, to the point that they occasionally washed her feet with their own hands. Garments were being made for the deceased and all else was being readied of which he had need. Meanwhile, the slave drinks every day and sings, giving herself over to pleasure.

§89: When the day arrived on which the man was to be cremated and the girl with him, I went to the river on which was his ship. I saw that they had drawn the ship out onto the shore, that they had erected four posts of birch wood and other wood, and that around the ship was made a structure like great ships' tents out of wood. Then they pulled the ship up until it was on this wooden construction. Then they began to come and go and to speak words, which I did not understand, while the man was still in his grave and had not yet been brought out. Then they brought a couch and put it on the ship and covered it with a mattress of Greek brocade. Then came an old woman whom they call the Angel of Death, and she spread upon the couch the furnishings mentioned. It is she who has charge of the clothes-making and arranging all things, and it is she who kills the girl slave. I saw that she was a strapping old woman, fat and threatening.

When they came to the grave, they removed the earth from above the wood, then the wood, and took out the dead man clad in the garments in which he had died. I saw that he had grown black from the cold of the earth. They had put *nabīd,* fruit, and a pandora* in the grave with him. They removed all that. The dead man did not smell bad and only his color had changed. They dressed him in trousers, stockings, boots, a tunic, and a caftan of brocade with gold

*[A type of stringed musical instrument, possibly related to a mandolin or lyre. —*Trans.*]

buttons. They put a hat of brocade and fur on him. They carried him into the pavilion on the ship. They seated him on the mattress and propped him up with cushions. They brought *nabīd,* fruits, and fragrant plants, which they put with him, then bread, meat, and onions, which they placed before him. Then they brought a dog, which they cut in two and put in the ship. Then they brought his weapons and placed them by his side. Then they took two horses, ran them until they sweated, then cut them into pieces with a sword and put them into the ship. Then they took two cows, which they likewise cut to pieces and put in the ship. Next they killed a rooster and a hen and threw them in. The girl slave who wished to be killed went here and there and into each of their tents, and the master of each tent had sexual intercourse with her and said, "Tell your lord I have done this out of love for you."*

Commentary on §89: The ship was pulled ashore onto a platform and protected from tipping over by means of support poles. Below the platform a space was probably reserved for the firewood for the cremation. The tent on the deck of the ship recalled the tent-shaped burial chamber made from wooden planks† in which the deceased, outfitted with everything he needed, would begin his final ship voyage. He had already been kept in the proper mood by drink, food, and a musical instrument for a ten-day waiting period in a provisional earthen grave. The definitive outfitting and preparation he received for the ship burial was stately. The two horses that were to accompany him were slaughtered at the moment of their greatest display of strength, so a maximum of vitality was preserved for them for the next world. Things proceeded in a similar way with the killing of the female slave (see §90). The sexual claims of the dead slaveholder

---

*[Or "for him," as in Smyser's translation; the exact original meaning here is ambiguous. —*Trans.*]

†Like the tent-shaped wooden burial chamber of the Gokstad ship in the museum at Bygdøy.

on his female slave were represented by the living companions of the deceased at the outset of following him into death. At any rate, this was the sense of the claims that they spoke aloud on this occasion. Although not too much can be clarified grammatically concerning the phrase "out of love for you"—does it refer to the female slave, or to the deceased?—the situation is clear enough: the slave girl, too, had vital claims on life and the living, which could not be "lived out" on account of her premature and impending death. Premature death was dangerous for both the deceased and for the living: a life that was not fully lived prevented the deceased from finding peace in the next world. It compelled the deceased back into the world of the living, where he could attempt to satisfy his hunger for life and for the living in a perverse manner as a revenant.* The sexual permissiveness granted to the slave girl for the last ten days of her life thus further served to relinquish, in advance and in a concentrated way, any sexual claims for the unlived life, thus prophylactically hindering any existence as a revenant after death. The "Angel of Death" who would kill the girl behaved like a slave herself (see §90) and hardly like a priestess (as is sometimes claimed).

§90: Friday afternoon they led the slave girl to a thing that they had made which resembled a door frame. She placed her feet on the palms of the men and they raised her up to overlook this frame. She spoke some words and they lowered her again. A second time they raised her up and she did again what she had done; then they lowered her. They raised her a third time and she did as she had done the two times before. Then they brought her a hen; she cut off the head, which she threw away, and then they took the hen and put it in the ship. I asked the interpreter what she had done. He answered,

---

*Compare Goethe's ballad "Die Braut von Korinth" (The Bride of Corinth) or Adolphe Adam's ballet *Giselle,* which is based on Heinrich Heine's story of the "Wilis." [The origins of the Wilis, a sirenlike female ghost who torments mortal men, ultimately trace back to the Slavic mythological figure of the *Vila.* —*Trans.*]

"The first time they raised her she said, 'Behold, I see my father and mother.' The second time she said, 'I see all my dead relatives seated.' The third time, she said, 'I see my master seated in Paradise, and Paradise is beautiful and green; with him are men and boy servants. He calls me. Take me to him.'" Now they took her to the ship. She took off the two bracelets which she was wearing and gave them both to the old woman called the Angel of Death, who was to kill her; then she took off the two finger rings which she was wearing and gave them to the two girls who served her and were the daughters of the woman called the Angel of Death. Then they raised her onto the ship, but they did not make her enter the pavilion.

The men came with shields and sticks. She was given a cup of *nabīd;* she sang at taking it and drank. The interpreter told me that she in this fashion bade farewell to all her girl companions. Then she was given another cup; she took it and sang for a long time while the old woman incited her to drink up and go into the pavilion, where her master lay. I saw that she was distracted; she wanted to enter the pavilion but put her head between it and the boat. Then the old woman seized her head and made her enter the pavilion, and she entered with the servant girl. Thereupon the men began to strike with the sticks on the shields so that her cries could not be heard and the other slave girls would not be frightened and seek to escape death with their masters. Then six men went into the pavilion and each had intercourse with the girl. Then they laid her at the side of her master; two held her feet and two held her hands; the old woman known as the Angel of Death re-entered and looped a cord around her neck, and gave the crossed ends to the two men for them to pull. Then she approached her with a broad-bladed dagger, which she plunged between her ribs repeatedly, and the men strangled her with the cord until she was dead.

Commentary on §90: The construction, which the female slave is lifted up onto, is a magical scaffold. Similar magical scaffolds (*seið-hjallr*) are known to us from North Germanic literature: these are high platforms upon which sorceresses can perform rites and see above the normal realm of perception.* In this example, the female slave, who is already intoxicated from the beer, achieves a glimpse of the next world. A rooster is a messenger of the new day and of new life, and the same is probably true of the hen (see §89) when it is sacrificed by (or for) a woman.[13] The display of noise is part of the event—it is not done in order to drown out the screaming but rather to hinder the return of the deceased. Our present-day church bells (sounding the death toll) have the same function, as does the salvo fired at the graveside of a soldier. The killing of the female slave at the moment of the greatest display of vitality— sexual intercourse, through which the living men again represent the deceased—secures for her (and for her master) the greatest vitality in the next world (see §89). Concerning similar reports of sexual excess, Jacob Grimm claims that "[s]uch an abomination would have been a foreign custom to the ancient Norse and ancient Germans."

§91: Then the closest relative of the dead man, after they had placed the girl whom they have killed beside her master, came, took a piece of wood which he [the relative] had lighted at a fire, and walked backward with the back of his hand toward the boat and his face turned toward the people, with one hand holding the kindled stick and the other covering his anus, being completely naked, for the purpose of setting fire to the wood that had been made ready beneath the ship. Thereupon the flames engulfed the wood, then the ship, the pavilion, the man, the girl, and everything in the ship. A powerful, fearful wind began to blow so that the flames became fiercer and more intense.

§92: One of the Rūs was at my side, and I heard him speak to the interpreter, who was present. I asked the interpreter what he said.

---

*The sorcerer/sorceress sits elevated upon a magical scaffold or dwells in a high tower (a magical tower), like the Germanic prophetess Veleda.

He answered: "He said, 'You Arabs are fools.'" "Why?" I asked him. He said: "You take the people who are most dear to you and whom you honor most and you put them in the ground, where insects and worms devour them. We burn him in a moment, so that he enters Paradise at once." Then he began to laugh uproariously. When I asked him why he laughed, he said: "His lord, for love of him, has sent the wind to bring him away in an hour." And actually an hour had not passed before the ship, the wood, the girl, and her master were nothing but cinders and ashes.

Then, in the place where there had been the ship, which they had drawn up out of the river, they constructed something like a small round hill, in the middle of which they erected a great post of birch wood on which they wrote the name of the man and the name of the Rūs king, and they departed.

Commentary on §91: Nudity is a widespread element in cultic funerary rites. Among other things, it signifies a casting off and severing of ties. as well as a cultic identification with the deceased, who has to free himself or herself of ties to the world of the living (see §87). Here the deceased relative therefore was approached either from behind or with the back turned, in order to avoid being possessed or fetched away by the dead. Yet the naked back turned to the deceased necessitated that the rear end was covered, because exposing this area of the body to someone is generally known as a gesture of abuse.

Commentary on §92: The previously mentioned epic of *Beowulf* from the West Germanic area begins with the description of a ship burial (see commentary on §87) and concludes with the description of a royal cremation and the erection of a grave mound over the burned remains of the corpse and the burial offerings.[14]

§93: He [Ibn Faḍlān] said: It is the custom of a king of the Rūs to have with him in his palace four hundred men, the bravest of companions and those on whom he can rely. These are the men who die with him and let themselves be killed for him. Each has a female slave who serves him, washes his head, and prepares all that he eats and drinks, and he also has another female slave with whom he sleeps. These four hundred men sit about the king's throne, which is immense and encrusted with fine precious stones. With him on the throne sit forty female slaves destined for his bed. Occasionally, he has intercourse with one of them in the presence of the companions of whom we have spoken, without coming down from the throne. When he needs to answer the call of nature, he uses a basin. When he wants to ride out, his horse is brought up to the throne and he mounts. If he wishes to dismount, he rides up so that he can dismount on to the throne. He has a lieutenant who commands his troops, makes war upon his enemies, and plays his role vis-à-vis his subjects.

Commentary on §93: Here we are shown something about the social structure of this Viking society. Typical is the institution of the warband,* which is well attested in the Germanic world. The warrior elite surrounding the king of the Rūs and the king himself appear to be unmarried in our sense of the word; as a sexual outlet they have female slaves. Large halls, in which kings live together with their hall companions are described clearly in North and West Germanic sources.[15] The custom that the king not touch the earth, which would weaken and degrade him, is otherwise unknown among the Germanic peoples. Nevertheless, in his *History of the Danes* (written ca. 1200), the Christian Danish chronicler Saxo Grammaticus (d. 1216 CE) attributes bad character to a heathen Swedish king who climbs down from his horse to pick up a piece of gold jewelry on the ground. Apparently this damaged his reputation.[16]

Some Conclusions

What sort of society has Ibn Faḍlān described for us? The Rūs on the Volga were Vikings (Varangians). They engaged in trade and warfare,

---

*[German *Gefolgschaft*, "warband, retinue." —*Trans.*]

living as predatory traders. They raided in one place and sold their booty in another. They were organized as a *Männerbund;** they supplied their need for females by raiding, rape, and enslavement. The warrior elite lived permanently around the king; they were bound to him in a life-and-death relationship of the warband. This warband relationship seems to be the strongest of the social ties that held together this tightly knit society. The following-into-death rite of the female slave, which naturally is based upon a social connection, did not serve the cohesion of the warband society (of the living) but rather provided for the dead lord in the next world.

Sketched out for us are the basic contours of the procedure for our approach to Germanic religion and, along with it, the structure of the book. We first must ask how it came about that a Germanic group was in the Volga region in the tenth century and what sort of people these were. That can be meaningfully answered only through an overview of the history of the Germanic tribes. In order to make Ibn Faḍlān's depiction more understandable to us, we must deal with the social structure of Germanic communities. Along with this, we must examine the values that these Germanic societies developed. Only then can we begin to discuss the rites, powers, and myths—in other words, the religious elements—that correspond to such a social system and its order of values.

---

*[Literally, "men's confraternity," a warband bound by sworn allegiances to its lord or leader. The German term *Männerbund* (plural *Männerbünde*) is often used in the scholarly literature. —*Trans.*]

A Brief History of the Germanic Tribes[1]

Language and Name

We understand the term *Germanic peoples* to refer to speakers of Germanic languages, and *Germanic languages* to refer to the branch of languages that differentiated itself from related language groups of the Indo-European type by undergoing the so-called Germanic sound shift. This sound shift affected certain consonants. By way of example, in the Negau helmet inscription—HARIGASTITEIVA—we find the cognate of Iranian *kara*, "army," in the Germanic word *hari-*, with the initial *k* appearing as *h* (pronounced *ch*). The cognate of Latin *deus* (from Old Latin **deivos*, "god") is evident in the Germanic word *teiva*, with the initial *d* appearing as *t*.*

---

*[Reconstructed words and roots from proto-Germanic and proto-Indo-European are from here on preceded by an asterisk to indicate that these forms are not historically attested but are rather the product of careful reconstruction using the comparative method of historical linguistics and based on the evidence of cognates in the descendant languages. The Germanic word *teiva* of the Negau helmet inscription would, for example, derive from the proto-Germanic **tīwaz*, which in turn derives from proto-Indo-European **deiwos*. Because the Latin word *deus* ultimately shares this same source, it is therefore cognate—related in origin—to the Germanic term. The Latin word has an earlier, intermediary form in **deivos*, which is unattested in the nominative singular (hence the asterisk) but does appear in its accusative plural form, *deivos*, on the so-called Duenos vase, dated to ca. 550 BCE. —*Trans.*]

The ancient Germanic language territory can be divided into branches, with the words for *white* serving as a vocabulary reference.

BRANCHES OF THE ANCIENT GERMANIC LANGUAGE

South Germanic		North Germanic	East Germanic
Ingvaeonic *(West Germanic)*	*Old High German* Franconian	*West Norse* Old Norse Old Icelandic	Gothic (Vandalic Burgundian Rugian Skirian)
Anglo-Saxon (ancestor of English)	Bavarian Alemannic		
Old Low Franconian (ancestor of Dutch)	(Langobardic) (ancestor of modern German)	*East Norse* Old Danish Old Swedish	(now extinct)
Old Saxon (ancestor of Low German)		(ancestors of Norwegian, modern Icelandic, Danish, Swedish)	
hwīt	*(h)wīȝ*	*hvítr*	*ƕeits*
(modern English *white*)	(modern German *weiß*)	Swedish *vit*, Danish *hvid*	

The term *Germani* (which we translate loosely as "Germanic peoples") is the Roman designation for a specific group of peoples with a common language and culture, which formed a definite border against the Roman expansion efforts in the north. The Latin word *Germani* means "having the same origin, related, of a type"—and that simply could be the translation of a Germanic self-designation, which then would have sounded like **swēbōz* (from the root **swē-* "[one's] own, trusted").[2] The self-designation of *one* Germanic tribal confederation, the Suebi (the origin of the later name Swabian), as those who "belong together," thus in Latin translation became Germani, which was then used as a name for the *entire group* of peoples. This is similar to the situation today in which the Swiss refer to all Germans with the term Schwaben (Swabians)—but it is also probably the case, as with so many other place-names and designations for peoples, that the exact origin and meaning of Germani can no longer be determined, and any attempts at interpretation must remain pure speculation.

The Germanic Migrations

The Germanic peoples first entered the consciousness of the Roman world in the year 105 BCE, when two Roman armies were wiped out by the Ingvaeonic Cimbri at Arausio (Orange). The Cimbri, together with the Teutoni (whose Germanic origin is doubtful), were allegedly pressured by a flash flood into leaving their settlements on Jutland and moving together into the Mediterranean region in search of a new dwelling place. Under Germanic pressure, the Celts—who at one time even occupied all of southern Germany to the Central German Uplands, all of northwest Germany to the Weser River, and Bohemia (Bojohaemum) in the east—began to withdraw to the west. Suebian Marcomanni moved into Bohemia and adopted the name of the former Celtic inhabitants, the Bojer, as Baiern (*Bajowarjōz, "inhabitants of Bojer land"). Caesar was indirectly responsible for the further advance of the Germanic peoples: as a result of his victories over the Celtic Helvetii (at Bibracte in 58 BCE) and over Vercingetorix (in 52 BCE), Gaul became a Roman province and the Rhine became the eastern border of the Celtic tribes, while the Germanic tribes streamed to the other side of the Rhine. At a battle in the Teutoburg forest in the year 9 CE, three Roman legions under the command of Varus were destroyed by the Cheruscii (allied at the time with the Marcomanni) who were led by Arminius. In addition to historical accounts, the event is also documented epigraphically: a Roman gravestone from Xanten names a certain Caelius from Bologna who, as commander of the XVIIIth Legion, "fell in the Varus battle" (*occidit bello variano*) at the age of fifty-three and a half.

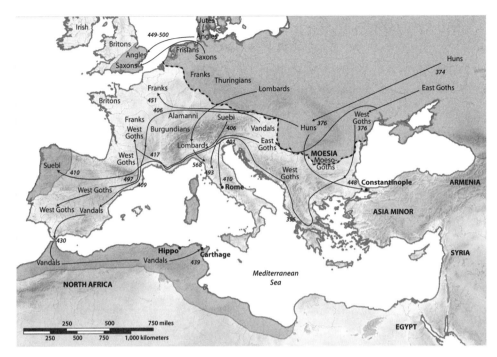

Germanic migrations in the fourth and fifth centuries CE. This map illustrates a number of the important ethnic-migrational movements mentioned in the text. It provides some general dates as well as the settled locations of various ethnic groups. The dashed line—which follows the geographical boundary of the Rhine and Danube Rivers—corresponds to the old border between the Roman Empire and the barbarian territory of Greater Germania (with Germanic and other ethnic groups situated to the north and east of the border). This map is only intended to give a simplified view of what were, in reality, far more complicated historical events. —*Trans.*

Why did the Germanic tribes exert pressure on the Celts? As early as the second century BCE, the Xiongnu (Huns) from the borders of China had begun to expand to the west and in doing so unleashed a whole chain reaction of population shifts and migrational movements. As a result, after the first century BCE, the Scythians (Śakas) and other peoples were pushed toward India. Circa 370–376 CE the Huns defeated Ermanaric, the East Gothic king, at the Black Sea. This in turn became the trigger for the major Germanic *Völkerwanderung* (tribal-ethnic migration). The West Goths pushed toward Italy, where Alaric captured Rome in 410. Alaric is said to be buried in Busento near Cosenza; the burial is described in August von Platen's ballad "Das

Grab im Busento" (The Grave in Busento). A small group of the West Goths did not take part in the migration; they retained their dwelling places in Moesia (on the southern bank of the Lower Danube), thus their name: Moeso-Goths.* The main troop of West Goths migrated from Italy to the Iberian Peninsula. In Italy the East Goths followed in their footsteps under the command of Theodoric (498–526). In Ravenna, Theodoric's tomb—with its domed roof constructed from a single monolith—and the ruins of his residence can still be seen today. Together with the Alans (members of an Iranian people whose descendants are the present-day Ossets in the Caucasus) the Vandals crossed over from Spain to North Africa. The church father Augustine died in 430, when the Vandals besieged Hippo (in present-day Algeria). In 449, Angles and Saxons (and Jutes) from the Continent began their invasion of Britain, subjugating the Celtic population and establishing Germanic kingdoms.

Starting in 874, the settlement of Iceland began in Norway, shortly after West Norse seafarers first reached the island. When they found the island it was already inhabited by Irish Christians, who departed shortly afterward. About a hundred years later the Icelander Erik the Red stepped ashore on Greenland. Around the year 1000, his son Leif reached America (Vinland).[3] If the so-called Parahyba Inscription (dated to the fourth or fifth century BCE) is genuine, however, then West Semitic traders already had trading outposts in South America before the middle of the first millennium BCE, and bold Leif and his crew can no longer be called the "discoverers" of America.[†]

---

*[Also referred to in German scholarly literature as the *Kleingoten* (Little Goths)—not in reference to their physical size, but rather to their status as the remnant of a larger group. —*Trans.*]

†[The Parahyba or Paraíba Inscription was allegedly transcribed in the early 1870s from a stone found at Pouso Alto in Brazil (and since claimed to be lost). The text describes the journey of a group of Phoenician Canaanites who inadvertently sailed to the New Shore of the American continent. The inscription is widely seen as a forgery. Nevertheless, there will probably always remain an open question as to the identity of who really first "discovered" America. —*Trans.*]

At this point the Germanic groups, which were on the move, were no longer entire ethnic clans and tribal confederations but rather bands of armed young men under the direction of a leader. As predatory traders organized in a *Männerbund,* these Vikings (*víkingar*) or Normans (Northmen) made use of the bays (*vík*) of the seas and waterways, raiding, murdering, plundering, robbing, raping, enslaving, and buying and selling. As a result they became not only the terror of the medieval world but also the greatest spreaders of cultural goods.

Already, before the ninth century CE, East Norse Vikings called Varangians ("oath comrades," from *vár,* or "vow") ventured to Russia. Another descriptive word for the Varangians, Rūs (which may mean "oar people"), provided the name for the Russians and their country. They traveled with their swift, lightweight boats on the large waterways (the Dnieper, the Don, the Volga) and across the Black Sea to Byzantium, where they were employed as the elite troupe and bodyguard of the Byzantine emperor.

The Persian poet Nizāmī reports a raid by the Rūs who traveled across the Caspian Sea to Abkhazia. He describes their lust for robbery and their blind destructive rage, their mode of battle (attack by night), and even a berserker (an elite warrior who, by using certain specific ecstatic techniques, was able to put himself into a state in which he seemed to be practically invulnerable).[4]

To the relief of the besieged Caucasian population, we know from another Oriental source[5] that the Rūs suffered a dysentery epidemic and were able to be eliminated. The Viking Rurik (the name derives from Hróðrekr, meaning "he whose renown is mighty") is regarded as the founder of the Russian empire; many Russian princely lineages trace back to him in a direct line their descent. His son Igor, the grand prince of Kiev, was slain by members of a subjugated tribe of Slavs after he wanted to collect the same tribute from them twice. His wife, Olga, or Helga, avenged his death in true Viking style when, in a breach of hospitality, she had those who were responsible burned alive (*brenna inni*) in a bathhouse and others slain at a beer-drinking feast. Then, with an army, she besieged the capital of the rebellious tribe, but offered the tribe peace on the condition that every household should compensate her with three sparrows and three doves as an expiatory payment. Having collected these, she ordered that pieces of burning tinder be attached to the birds before setting them free. Carrying the embers, they flew back to their original nests—and soon the entire city was in flames.[6] Olga took over rulership and was baptized in 955 in Byzantium; her Christian name is Helena. Olga/Helga/Helena thus became the actual mother of the Russian empire, which the Rurikids governed until 1598.[7] Many beloved Russian names are of Viking origin: Igor (Ingvar[d]), Oleg (Helgi), Olga (Helga), Wladimir (Waldemar), and so on. Since the fifteenth century the Cossacks have been the spiritual descendants of the Vikings: they made use of *Männerbund*-type lifestyles, a *comitatus* existence,* abduction of women, predatory trade, nighttime attacks, and light and fast boats. They expanded the borders of the Russian empire far to the south and to the east (Siberia).

The Vikings ravaged practically the entire Continent along with its accompanying insular areas (the British Isles, Sicily, the Balearic Islands). In addition, there was talk of an attempt to gain a foothold in Asia (in the Caucasus). Just as suddenly, however, by the turn of the eleventh to the twelfth centuries, the din quieted: the Vikings became Christians, established political systems, and erected magnificent Norman cathedrals, a building style that led from the Romanesque to the Gothic. This brings up the topic of the Christianization of the Germanic peoples, which we have yet to consider.

The causes that spurred the Germanic peoples on their earlier migrations were largely of a historical nature, but what caused the bands of young Vikings to set out on such an epidemic scale? Was it simply lust for adventure? That was certainly a part of it. In northern Germanic tradition,[8] the start of the Viking excursions was marked by the Battle of Brávellir (on the coast of East Götaland)—the greatest battle of the

---

*[Latin *comitatus* is a designation for a raiding warband or retinue. The Roman historian Tacitus, for example, uses the term in reference to certain Germanic societies in his *Germania*. —*Trans.*]

north, described by Saxo in almost apocalyptic terms and one in which power relations were newly established with the victory of the Swedes over the Danes. In this case the beginning of the Viking movements was in the eighth century—but what about the cause, or better, the causes, of these movements?

One of the primary causes seems to be of a religious nature and relates to the cult of the dead. An Icelandic saga from the thirteenth century starts off with a father inciting his son, who is an "ash lad" (we would say a young bird that won't leave the nest), finally to leave his warm home, set out on his own two feet, and seek his fortune in the world at large. The scene takes place in the eleventh century. The father, Ketil, says to his son, Thorstein:

> The behaviour of young men today is not what it was when I was young. . . . It was once the custom of powerful men, kings or earls—those who were our peers—that they went off raiding and won riches and renown for themselves, *and such wealth* [plunder] *did not count as part of any legacy, nor did a son inherit it from his father; rather was the money to lie in the tomb alongside the chieftain himself.** And even if the sons inherited the lands, they were unable to sustain their high status, if honour counted for anything, unless they put themselves and their men at risk and went into battle, thereby winning for themselves, each in his turn, wealth and renown—and so following in the footsteps of their kinsmen.[9]

This then means that the "portion for the deceased," which the father takes with him to the grave (in the form of gold, silver, and valuable objects), is so large that the remainder (consisting of land and some associated moveable wealth) bequeathed to the descendants offers no sufficient basis for livelihood. Thus the descendants are forced, along

*[The italics for emphasis are from Hasenfratz; bracketed clarifications to the cited English translation are mine. —*Trans.*]

with similarly fated companions of the same age, to go on raiding missions, "to go a-viking," and in this way, to win their fortune. Because what they gain (plunder) then accompanies them into the grave, they in turn pass on this same way of life to their own descendants. This may bring to mind the passage in Ibn Faḍlān's travel report, which describes the dividing of the Rūs chieftain's estate: one-third of his wealth goes to those who remain alive, but the main portion (two-thirds) is used for the funeral and related cult activities for the deceased and is thus kept from any use by the living.

The Christianization of the Germanic peoples began with the Moeso-Goths. The Bible was translated into Gothic under their bishop Wulfila (whose name literally means "little wolf," d. 383 CE), who probably did the translation himself. For a sample of the text we can look at the first part of the Lord's Prayer.

Atta unsar
Þu in himinam
weihnai namo þein
qimai in þiudinassus þeins
wairþai wilja þeins
swe in himina
jah ana airþai[10]

Our father [compare dialectal modern Alemannic
    German Ätti, "father"],
You in the heavens!
May your name be holy [compare German geweiht,
    "consecrated"],
Your empire [literally, "rule over the people"] come,
Your will be manifest [literally, "turn out to be";
    compare German werde, "become"]
as in heaven (so) too on earth.

The approximate end point for the conversion of the Germanic peoples came about with the conversion of the Icelanders to Christianity in the year 1000. According to the account in the Icelandic sources,[11] the following chain of events took place: the Norwegian king Olaf Tryggvason, a former Viking who had been baptized, installed as his court chaplain a man with the German name Thangbrand. This man had killed another who sought a dispute with him over his Irish slave girl. In addition to this, the chaplain began to involve himself in Viking expeditions in order to augment his income from the priesthood. When the king heard about this, he disciplined Thangbrand by transferring him to Iceland and giving him the task of converting the Icelanders. After the zealous missionary had slain a number of men who mocked him, he returned to Norway. Angry at the failure of the venture, King Olaf interned all Icelanders who were staying in Norway. Two Icelanders who had been baptized earlier by Thangbrand, Hjalti and Gizur, promised the king they would make another attempt to convert their countrymen in Iceland if the king would release the interned Icelanders in Norway. The king agreed, and Hjalti and Gizur sailed home to Iceland. There, they gathered up the men who were loyal to them and rode, armed, to the Althing, the annual national assembly. The opponents of the church likewise armed themselves. The gathering was on the verge of degenerating into a battle between Christians and heathens, with unforeseeable consequences. The lawspeaker (*lǫgsǫgu-maðr*), whose job it was to recite the law code aloud at the Thing, the annual popular assembly, was asked to mediate the situation. Thorgeir the Lawspeaker, who was himself a heathen, said nothing. He rested the remainder of the day until the following one, and then he opened the assembly. The parties declared themselves ready to accept his arbitration. Thorgeir announced that all those people who were still unbaptized at that point should be baptized. The exposure of children and the eating of horsemeat (sacrificial meat) should continue according to the old ways, and heathen sacrifices should be allowed to continue if they take place in private. Public sacrifices, however, should be punished with exile for three years.

The arbitration was accepted by both parties. It was said that Thorgeir had been bribed beforehand by the Christians.

The conversion of the remaining Germanic peoples, especially those in the southern territories, took place during the period between the two great migrational movements, or, more specifically, between the beginning of the Migration Age and the Viking Age. The great missionary in the German-speaking realm was the Anglo-Saxon Wynefrið, better known as Bonifatius (Boniface), the "apostle to the Germans." He was killed by heathen Frisians in 754, and he lies buried in the cathedral at Fulda. Today we can see in the cathedral museum a reliquary with his head, and on display in the Hessian Regional Library is the bundle of papers that Boniface held up defensively in front of his head before he was dealt the deadly blow.

We must note that the conversion of the Germanic peoples was a relatively peaceful process.[12] Above all, the church offered the Germanic peoples access to what was, in their eyes, a superior culture: a culture of writing and books, which granted them access to the worlds of the Mediterranean and classical antiquity. The situations in which the use of violence occurred came about when Christianity was implemented by rulers for the building and consolidation of unifying and centralizing power structures, and it is only in this context that we should view the forced conversion of the Saxons by Charlemagne. The forced conversion of the Saxons is exactly what is repeatedly offered as proof for the claim that Christianity was imposed upon the Germanic peoples with violence and that it is fundamentally alien to the "Germanic essence." This thesis was advanced by the chief ideologue of the Third Reich, Alfred Rosenberg, as well as by Hitler, and had its earlier promoters even before these two promulgated the idea. Today it is again advocated by neopagan groups (which are partly intertwined with the New Age)[13] and in books with characteristic titles such as *Europas eigene Religion* (Europe's Own Religion) by Sigrid Hunke[14] and *Der Glaube der Ahnen* (The Faith of the Ancestors) by Klaus Bemmann.[15]

The question of whether a religion resonates with—or is alien to—

the "essence" of a group of people (in this case, the Germanic peoples) cannot be decided by a scholar of religion, because for such a scholar the term *Germanic* refers simply to a linguistic community, and we must reject as unscientific "determinations of essence." In the best-case scenario, a specific religion (the Germanic, the Christian) and its development can be adequately described and that is all. We should also recognize, however, that it was precisely in the Germanic-speaking realm where Christianity experienced a deepening and unfolding to a degree that probably occurred in no other linguistic area. Various figures come to mind, such as Gottschalk, a Saxon of the first generation after conversion, with his doctrine of double predestination; Anselm of Canterbury, of Langobardic stock, the "father of scholasticism," with his satisfaction doctrine (the doctrine of the work of Christ); and Thomas Aquinas, the powerful systematizer of Christian theology, who was of German-Norman heritage. In addition we must note the reformers Martin Luther and Huldrych Zwingli, the Catholic writer and mystic Matthias Joseph Scheeben in the nineteenth century, and the reformed theologian Karl Barth in the twentieth century. If all of these people are taken into consideration with regard to "determinations of essence," we must conclude that Christianity has resonated, and resonates, with a "Germanic essence" in a very special way.

Society and Its Values (Sociography and Axiology)

The Social Classes[1]

An Eddic poem from the thirteenth century reports to us in mytho-poetic form about the origination of the classes[2]—or, more specifically, about the slaves and the three classes—and their functions. It is thus a myth of origins and a mirror of the class structure all in one.[3] The god Rígr (his name derives from the Celtic word for king), who is probably an emanation of Odin, travels throughout the land. He enjoys the hospitality of a childless married couple, sleeping three nights with the wife of the host (an example of so-called guest prostitution), and then he wanders on. After nine months the woman gives birth to a boy named Þræll (thrall). He grows up and marries a maiden named Þír (*þý*, "slave woman"). She does servant's work, and they propagate their lineage; from them is descended the race of thralls (servants). Rígr enjoys the hospitality of another childless married couple, sleeping three nights with the wife of the host, and then he wanders on. After nine months the woman gives birth to a son named Karl ("man of low class"; the word is cognate with "churl"). Karl grows up and finds a wife for himself. They have children and practice farming and crafts; from them is descended the race of freemen (the *karlar*). Rígr enjoys the hospitality of yet another childless married couple, sleeps three nights with the wife of the host, and then wanders on. After nine months she gives birth to a son named Jarl ("man of noble standing, chieftain, warrior"). Jarl grows up, hunts, fights, feuds, conquers land, and distributes treasures (is generous). He learns how to use the runes. He wins the daughter of Hersir (a word that means "regional military leader"), and they go off to live in contentment and pleasure; they have offspring. The youngest child is named Konr ungr ("young sproutling"). From his father he learns the art of magic, knowledge, strength, cunning, and skillfulness—he is bound to be a king (*konungr*).

The structure of Germanic society is trifunctional, as this tale relates, and in this sense, it corresponds to other Indo-European societies. The class of authority (rulers, priests) is represented in this myth by Konr ungr, the king (*konungr*). The class of force (warriors) is represented by Jarl, the nobleman; the class of producers (peasants, craftsmen) by Karl, the freeman. Below this order of classes, Þræll represents those who are unfree and who do not have inherent rights (slaves, servants). In ancient India this scheme corresponds to the three upper castes (*brahmans, kshatriyas, vaishyas*) and the contemptible, non-Aryan servants (*shudras*). In his conception of an ideal state, Plato differentiates among the rulers or philosophers, guards or helpers, and common people. The church's social doctrine in medieval Europe divided society into the three classes of *oratores* (those who pray), *bellatores* (those who fight), and *laboratores* (those who work). Martin Luther's conception of the classes is analogous, with a *Lehrstand* (learned class), *Wehrstand* (armed class), and *Nährstand* (food-producing class). In all of these systems the slaves, foreigners, unfree people, and the "dishonorable" are ranked below the scale and outside of the order. The trifunctional division of classes emerged again in the National Socialist state as dreamed of and schemed out by Alfred Rosenberg and Adolf Hitler. They had in mind an *Ordenstaat* (order-based state) ruled by an *Ordensrat* (order council) and the *Führer* who was elected from it,* based upon a *Leistungsadel* ("nobility of accomplishment," the broad elite of Party members as a middle stratum), supported by the *Volksgemeinschaft* (the "folk community," the great mass of the "ever sheeplike") and commanding over a labor army of "subjugated aliens," a "modern slave stratum."[4]

It is understandable that this trifunctionality reveals itself most clearly among peoples with a settled way of life. For nomadic tribes and mobile societies, certain functions in the structure may not be present. In the producer class this might be the case with the peasants, for example, though not with the craftsmen. The class system among Germanic societies was not as rigid and fixed as the one in India but was instead flexible and porous. A slave could become free through acts of bravery, a peasant could become a noble,[†5] and a noble could become a king. The porosity of the system is illustrated by the thirteenth-century tale of Gebe-Ref, which we will return to later in this chapter. Porosity is also ensured by a class-transcending system of social ties, the so-called *Männerbund*.

The Slaves

For the ancient Germanic peoples, the slave (originally from *slav:* an unfree person of Slavic origin) was an object. This is linguistically apparent from the fact that the Old Icelandic neuter word *man* denotes a quantity of slaves or a single female slave (compare the German secondary neuter form *das Mensch,* "cow, slut," as opposed to the primary masculine form *der Mensch,* "human being [of either sex]"). As an object, the slave could be bought, sold, used, misused, or killed—all according to necessity, desire, or mood. A slave was typically obtained as war booty. The old Germanic designations for slaves are still hidden

---

*[The word *order* is used here in the sense of an organization of people united by a common aim, such as in a knightly, religious, or fraternal order. —*Trans.*]

†As it states in the legendary Danish so-called Frothi's law.

in the modern German words *Schalk*, "joker," "rogue" (from Old High German *skalk*, "servant"), *Diener*, "servant," "valet" (compare Gothic *þius*, "servant," and Old Icelandic *þý*, "slave woman"), and *Welscher*, "Italian," "foreigner" (pejorative; compare Old English *wealh*, "slave from Wales," "servant"). The fundamental meanings of the words *slave* and *Welscher* suggest the original acquisition of slaves through military subjugation and capture of members of foreign ethnic groups, as we have already seen in the case of the Rūs.

Here are a few examples that illustrate some of the ways in which the Germanic peoples dealt with their slaves.

The thirteenth-century *Laxdœla saga* (Saga of the People of Laxardale) depicts the purchase of a slave woman at a market near the present-day city of Gothenburg, Sweden, in the tenth century.[6] When Hoskuld (a protagonist in the saga) goes out one evening with some men to enjoy himself in the market town, he sees a magnificent-looking tent that belongs to Gilli the Russian (recall our earlier discussions of the Rūs). Gilli asks what Hoskuld and his companions might be seeking. Hoskuld replies that he wants to buy a slave woman. The Russian pulls back a curtain dividing the interior of the tent. Behind it are seated twelve women. Hoskuld examines them closely and decides upon one. Gilli demands three times the normal price for her, namely three marks' weight in silver.* Hoskuld agrees, and the payment is weighed out. Hoskuld takes the woman with him and sleeps with her. The next morning, apparently pleased with her, he buys her new clothing.

The thirteenth-century *Egils saga* (Egil's Saga) depicts the demise of its hero, the Viking and farmer Egil, in southwestern Iceland at the end of the tenth century.[7] The aged Egil feels himself nearing his own death, and while everyone is asleep, he takes all his silver—two trunkfuls—

---

*At the current price of silver in 1991, when this chapter was written, this equaled approximately $84.33. [Dollar amount based on an averaged currency conversion for the year 1991, applied to Hasenfratz's original calculation of 144 German marks, which was based on June 25, 1991, rates from the Sparkasse bank in Bochum. —*Trans.*]

and calls two of his nephew's slaves (Egil is living with his nephew), orders them to fetch a horse, and rides off with the slaves. He has the slaves sink the trunks of silver in a bog. He then kills the servants and sinks them along with the treasure so that no one will discover where it is hidden. The next morning he heads home, leading the horse behind him. Soon afterward he dies and is buried in a mound with his weapons and clothing. This is how the cunning Egil securely keeps away from the living his portion for the deceased.

For freed slaves life was often more miserable than for working slaves. Deprived of sufficient economic support, freed slaves quickly became impoverished and their children did not survive. The oldest legal text from Norway, the eleventh-century Christian lawbook for the region of the Gulaþing, regulates the problem in this way: "If, however, the children [of someone released from slavery] find themselves impoverished, then they are 'ready to go to the grave' [*grafgangsmenn*]: a grave shall be dug in the churchyard and they shall be placed into it and allowed to die there [*oc setja þau þar i, oc lata þar deyja*]. The legal master [their former owner] shall take the one out that lives the longest and feed it [*þat,* neuter] from then on."*8

The Peasants and Craftsmen

In contrast to the free peasant, less notice is paid to the craftsman, because he does not work for himself but instead works for others. A bit of Eddic wisdom bluntly instructs:

> *Be neither a shoemaker nor a shaftmaker,*
> *for anyone but yourself;*
> *if the shoe is badly fitting or the spear is crooked,*
> *then a curse will be called down on you.*[9]

"Of the work done in service to the next man there is no trace,"

---

*Bracketed explanations are mine.

concludes an expert on the matter. He draws attention to the Old Icelandic word for work, *vinna* ("to win, conquer, take hold of, gain"), which, in its descriptive sense, refers less to a notion of honest industriousness on the part of the citizenry than it does to Viking plundering.[10]

The fact that talented, skilled craftsmen and ingenious technicians were at work among the Germanic peoples is proved by archaeological evidence directly from the Viking Age. The Viking ships are probably the most seaworthy vessels in the history of nautical science. In the Viking Museum in Haithabu/Hedeby ("heath settlement") in Schleswig, Germany, we can see a Viking warship, which was dredged up from the harbor as recently as 1979. Further, the glorious stave churches in Norway (Borgund, Heddal, Urnes) point to a long tradition of craftsmanship, artistry, and construction with wood.

The Warriors

The warriors were recruited from the youths of the peasant class and from the sons of the nobles. They were organized in terms of a *Männerbund,* gathering as a retinue around the king or the bold leader of a Viking undertaking.

At the age of twelve a young man was capable of bearing weapons. As long as he was in service to a king, the king would cater to and outfit him. Later on, the war booty was divvied up according to his competence in battle, or, in other words, according to the number of men he had killed. The retinue satisfied its need for females with slave women from the captured war booty. The royal hall was ruled by a strict pecking order, which manifested as a seating order. The bravest men sat above; the less competent had to settle for lower places at the table and were sometimes pelted with bones by those who sat higher up.[11]

Only someone fit for battle was a man in the full sense of the word. This is already evident from the poetic circumlocutions (kennings) for *man,* which include: Bidder to Battle, God of Weapons, Battle Tree, Tree of the Shield, and Tree That Desires the Storm of Arrows. Honorable activity consisted solely of war and fighting—all else was indolence.

Saxo, the Christian author of the *History of the Danes,* reports, half admiringly, about his heathen forebears: "In times past people believed that the supreme goal was a celebrity achieved not by dazzling riches but by hard activity in war. Illustrious men once made it their concern to pick quarrels, start up old feuds, loathe ease, choose soldiering in preference to peace. . . ."[12]

The Rulers

The ruling and the priestly functions were often difficult to distinguish from one another. This was the case with the Old Icelandic *goði* (a word that has an etymological relationship to English *god**), who was both a priest and a chieftain. The Old Norse word *jarl* refers not only to a nobleman of high rank (like the modern English *earl,* which describes a count), but also refers to a magically proficient rune expert (who probably also had cultic duties). In the myth we recounted earlier about the origin of the classes, the god Rígr teaches the runes to Jarl. Further, in the so-called runemaster formula that appears in many runic inscriptions, the writer uses the title *erilaʀ* (the proto-Norse form, which corresponds to the later Old Icelandic *jarl*), as in these examples: *ek erilaʀ rūnōʀ warītu* (I, the *jarl,* risted the runes); *i[k] uuīgaʀ eerilaʀ fāhidu uuīlald* (I, Vígr, the *jarl,* wrote the magical artwork).[†13]

Many Germanic ruling lineages trace their origin to the gods, especially to Odin or Frey. It can be said of a king, for example of King Aðils of Uppsala, that he was a devoted sacrificer to the gods.[14] Often, however, kings themselves were sacrificed. The Swedes are alleged to

---

*[Old Icelandic *goði,* "heathen priest," "chieftain," is a secondary derivation from the word *goð,* "heathen god," which is cognate to English *god.* A direct parallel to the Old Icelandic word is found in Gothic *gudja,* "priest." —*Trans.*]

†[*Risted* means "carved," "engraved." The term *to rist* was adopted into English by nineteenth-century scholars who studied Viking Scandinavia; it is an anglicization of the Old Norse verb *rísta,* which was often used to describe the carving of runes in wood, bone, or horn. It is etymologically related to the German word that Hasenfratz uses here, *ritzen.* Our English verb *to write* shares a common origin with all of these terms, as it also does with the word *warītu* in the inscription. —*Trans.*]

have once offered up King Óláfr to the god Odin, because he was not a great sacrificer and as a result was responsible for a bad year and famine in the land, and events proceeded in the same way for Dómaldi, the mythical king of the Swedes: following a number of years of misfortune and starvation, after which first oxen and then men had been offered up as sacrifices without success, the bad harvests were seen as the king's fault, and he himself was offered up for a good harvest (for a good year).[15] Also traditionally recorded and sung is the fate of the Norwegian king Víkarr, who is advised to go on a Viking trip during a lull in the weather. It is also advised that he should let himself be hanged in a faux sacrifice to obtain a good sailing wind. The rite goes awry due to Odin's intervention, and the king dies as a genuine sacrifice.[16] The king, because of his divine origins, is responsible for the healthy state of the land and the folk. The Germanic royal sacrifice could have very well provided the basis for an understanding of the work of Christ.

The mythical ideal king of the Germanic peoples was the king of the Danes named Frothi (Fróði, "the abundant one, the fertile one").[17] The learned Icelander Snorri Sturluson (d. 1241) identifies him with the god Frey in connection with Snorri's "euhemeristic" theory of the origin of the heathen gods: these were human beings who had later been deified (idolized). Frothi was said to have governed at the time of Augustus and to have been the first lawmaker.[18] Under him, the so-called Frothi peace was in effect: no one injured another; robbery and thievery were so unknown that in Jutland a gold ring could lie on a country road for three years without anyone taking it. Frothi was said to have had a "wishing mill": whoever was in a position to turn the millstone could mill (produce) anything that he desired. Frothi bought two captured giantesses as slaves who milled gold and peace for him day and night. Because he granted them no rest, in frustration they milled for him an army of enemies. As a result, Frothi was slain by a sea king (by Vikings), and his land was plundered. In this way the "golden age" of Frothi came to an end. In this case we are dealing with the primordial myth of a good, ancient king who, following a misstep, loses his paradisiacal luck and the peace of the primordial age. (This myth is similarly preserved in the Old Iranian tradition of King Yima.)

Generosity, which is an indispensable trait of rulers (kings, leaders) with respect to their retinues, is further discussed in the later section of this chapter titled "The Retinue."

The Stages of Life

The following sketch of the stages of life is drawn from a masculine and patriarchal perspective and reflects the nature of the sources, which are only marginally interested in portraying the lives of female members of society—even though the sources attest to a significant social influence on the part of the female gender. The ancient sources mention the names of Germanic seeresses (sorceresses, priestesses) such as Albruna, Veleda,[19] and Waluburg, of whom Veleda achieved fame through her political role at the Bataver uprising against the Romans on the Lower Rhine in the first century CE. Women certainly had an influential say in family matters. And some quarrels—which could have been reconciled among men with an atonement payment—were goaded by women into bloody feuds that could carry on for generations. It also cannot be claimed that Germanic women particularly distinguished themselves as "peace weavers"* (Kriemhild in the *Nibelungenlied* comes to mind!). Women did not only take on masculine values; they also often took them too far. The following portrait of life in terms of only masculine values is also justified throughout the Germanic sphere, because it reflects the dominance of male values among the various Germanic peoples.

Evidence stated here may serve for the description of Germanic societies, their values, and their religion on the whole.

---

*[This is an allusion to the Old English poetic term *freoðo-webbe*, "peace weaver," which is used in *Beowulf* as a synonym for "lady" in her idealized role, an ideal often honored in the breach by royal women. —*Trans.*]

Childhood

With the negative attitude of Germanic peoples toward what we call work on the one hand, and with a positive attitude toward the advancement of arms and warfare on the other, we shouldn't be surprised that children (boys) were seen as especially promising if they were lazy do-nothings ("ash lads") who didn't lift a finger to help out around the house.[20] Nor should we be surprised that a youth's best claim to fame was if he had already slain one or more men at a tender age, thus earning the pride of his mother.[21]

In Iceland a boy came of age at twelve, and he could ride with weapons to the Thing.[22]

Youth and Manhood

The mature and armed youth was free to join the retinue of a king or to go a-viking. If he had wealthy parents they would outfit him with a ship for this purpose. The young man then spent some years out on sea voyages, either in the service of a king or on private Viking expeditions. In either case, he lived as a warrior organized in a *Männerbund,* and he was sexually free.

Once a young man had amassed enough of a share of loot or goods from robbery and plunder, he returned to his father's estate or acquired his own property and married. He could settle down, because he now had an economic foundation that made him independent of a patriarchal inheritance. For as long as he felt himself to be sprightly and healthy, a farmer who had married and settled down would still continue to go on further Viking expeditions, which kept him away from his land for a certain amount of time.[23]

Old Age

If a man's days of vigor and fitness were over, and he became weak and unable to bear arms, he was no longer of value. The old man was shoved aside as useless and was even mocked for his weakness. The thirteenth-century *Egil's Saga* reports that the famed skald and fearsome Viking

Egil (who lived in the tenth century), having become weak in his old age, has to endure abuse from the women around him when he falls due to his frailty. (One of them declares to him: "You're completely finished, Egil.") Similarly, he must put up with being brusquely ordered by the cook (*matselja*)—in other words, by a servant—to get away from the fire where he keeps himself warm, because he is getting in the way of her work.[24] The famed Danish legendary hero Starkather (from Stark-hǫðr, meaning "strong in battle") prefers in his old age to be killed by a free man than to die in bed: "A young tree must be nourished, an ancient one hewn down. Whoever overthrows what is close to its fate and fells what cannot stand is an instrument of Nature." He allows himself voluntarily to have his head cut off by a blood avenger in order to avoid a death from old age and devoid of glory. Saxo provides us with a depiction of the scene.[25] A "straw death," or dying in bed, was considered shameful; Odin's Valhalla was reached only by those who died from weapons and wounds. Even on a deathbed a contemptible straw death could, however, be avoided if a man allowed himself to be "spear marked"—that is, cut with a spear (the weapon of Odin).[26]

The practice of killing the elderly, which is attested among the eastern and northern Germanic peoples,[27] was probably connected to the idea of sparing "useless mouths" from the fate of a straw death. In the thirteenth-century *Gautreks saga* (Gautrek's Saga), the elderly jump from a high cliff to their death in order to secure the survival of their descendants, and in doing so, they believe they are faring forth to meet Odin.[28]

The killing of the elderly is not a Germanic "specialty"; it was practiced in particular by the Siberian Chukchi people and given the name *kamitok*.

Mechanisms and Systems of Social Ties[29]

The Sib

In the word *Sib* (from a proto-Germanic base form *sibjō) we find the same Indo-European root—*s(w)e-* (suffixed with the element *-bh-*)—that appears in the Germanic tribal name of the Swabians and that means "[one's] own, related, trusted."* The Sib therefore denotes "that which belongs together." According to the Germanic view, the Sib was the group of freeborn people who were related to one another by blood and marriage. The underlying meaning of the Germanic word *friend* is "(family) relative." *Friend* (equivalent to modern German *Freund*) is linguistically related to the word *free* (German *frei*) and is also related to the German word for "peace," *Friede.*† All three words contain the proto-Germanic root **frī-*, which means "to love" (this sense is still present in the modern-day High Allemanic dialectal expression *es frīs Meitschi*, "a beloved girl"). Peace should thus have rule within the Sib, for the relatives were *friends* with one another. All who existed outside the Sib were potential enemies—including an unfree person, who could be slain at whim, without any obligation for compensation, by his or her master or any of the master's relatives. This tightly knit, familial sense of peace could cross the "aggression threshold" of the Germanic peoples: a minor incident might cost the life of someone alien to the Sib, which could lead to unceasing and bloody tribal feuds that escalated and dragged on for generations if the original slaying was not compensated for by paying *wergeld*‡ to the Sib that was harmed by it. This family-bound sense of peace meant the Germanic man sensed strife was lurking just outside the borders of the Sib. It also explains the specific endorsement of armed warfare as a means of distinguishing yourself in the social and political realm.

---

*[Sib (which translates the German word *Sippe* in the original text) is used in its anthropological sense to denote "a kinship group consisting of two or more lineages considered as being related" (*American Heritage Dictionary*). *Sib* and *Sippe* are in fact cognate words; the inherent sense of close-knit family ties is evident in our related and more common English term *sibling*. —*Trans.*]

†[German *Friede* has a cognate in the archaic English word *frith*, "peace." Compare, too, the note above regarding "peace weavers." —*Trans.*]

‡[*Wergeld*, which literally translates to "man payment" or "man compensation," refers to the Germanic legal custom by which a man's life was accorded a specific monetary value. If a person was killed without prior legal justification, the killer was theoretically obligated to compensate the family of the slain man with the requisite *wergeld*. —*Trans.*]

An expression of this "familialism" (although married relations were also included within the Sib peace) was the tendency for incestuous connections: the sexual partner was sought from among a person's own blood relations. Brother-sister marriage as a quasi-fixed institution for a Sib in Swedish Götaland is a motif in the thirteenth-century *Gautrek's Saga*.[30] And in the thirteenth-century *Saga of the Volsungs* a brother and sister conceive a son who—in more favorable circumstances—carries out blood vengeance by murdering their father and their brothers.*[31] The Norwegian law book for the territory of the Gulaþing and the later thirteenth-century Swedish Östgöta Law gave punishments for incest (Old Swedish *ætsku spiæll*) of Episcopal church penance for the man, with the Gulaþing imposing expulsion from the land for the man and woman if the fine of the church penance was not paid and the couple refused to separate.[32] We should also remember that among the Vanir, a group of Germanic fertility gods and goddesses, it was permitted to marry siblings: Njǫrðr and his sister (who may be Nerthus, deriving from an earlier form, *Nerþuz; see the discussion on pp. 109–10) conceived two divine children, Freyr and Freyja, who were, in turn, sexually involved with one another.[33] The erotically tinged love between brother and sister in German folktales may in some way be a further illustration of the strong brother-sister relationship within the Germanic Sib.

In ancient Iran the marriage of siblings (along with other incestuous relationships) was not only allowed but also was religiously sanctioned.

In subsequent sections we will examine mechanisms and systems of social ties that are: (1) capable of extending peace or essential elements of peace, both as it governs within the Sib and outwardly, to those who are not part of the Sib; and that are (2) capable of insuring a state of peace that transcends the peace of the Sib. These mechanisms and systems include the fosterage of children, oath brotherhood, hospitality

---

*The composer Richard Wagner took up the theme of brother-sister incest in his opera *Die Walküre* ("Bride and sister you are to your brother—so blossoms then the Volsungs' blood!").

to guests, gift giving, the *Männerbund,* the retinue, and the cultic society. They are capable of development and can become the basis of further analogous mechanisms and systems. They can also become linked among themselves to new mechanisms and systems, for they are themselves already partially the result of analogy and "networking." Questions regarding which of these mechanisms and systems of social ties are original (primary) and which are later developments (secondary) need not concern us here.

Fosterage

In the north it was a frequently practiced custom to take a child (usually at age seven) from his parents' home and place him in the home of another family that was not exactly of equal birth in terms of rank. This fosterage forged ties between the parents and the foster parents and among the children of both families. The foster child and the children of the foster parents had a relationship to one another like that of brother or sister; often marriages came about between foster siblings.

Among the Sawi tribe on the West Irian islands in Indonesia, fosterage is the basic outward tie that makes possible all further outward connections. As long as the foster child (*tarop tim,* "peace child") lives with the foster parents, the tribes (village communities) of the parents and foster parents are bound to one another in peaceful community.

Oath Brotherhood

Oath brotherhood (sworn or blood brotherhood) forged the same ties as those that arose for foster siblings through fosterage. This is evident because both institutions are not specifically distinguished from one another in terminology: the term *fóstbrœðralag* (foster brotherhood) is also used as a description for oath or blood brotherhood. The only difference was that oath brotherhood came about between male and mature members of different Sibs. When the rite of the celebratory swearing of brotherhood included the mixing of blood from both parties, it was termed *blood brotherhood.* The participants let their blood drip into their footprint in the ground, and thus the two became mixed. In tandem with this, the two usually walked under a cutout strip of turf, which was still connected to the ground and was held up by spears. The rite signified that they were indissolubly bound to one another and newly born from the same womb (the earth). Sometimes the blood brothers swore they would even follow one another into death: if one died, the other would be buried with him.

The mixing of spittle could occur instead of the mixing of blood, if we believe what Snorri Sturluson tell us. He describes a "spittle treaty" of this sort, which seals the peace between the two classes of Norse gods, the Æsir and the Vanir.[34] In any case, blood and spit are both types of "soul conveyors" and are powerful substances. A union through the mixing of blood or spit signified a joining of life and fate between two people.

Hospitality to Guests

The foreigner who had found reception as a guest (in Old High German and Middle High German, the word *gast* still had the sense of "foreigner, enemy") under a roof—which was not something that could always be taken for granted—enjoyed family friendship for a certain amount of time (three nights was proper), and secured shelter, food, and safe escort. Family friendship could also include the privilege of sleeping with the wife or daughter in the house, a custom that is denigrated with the ugly and incorrect term *guest prostitution*. It has nothing to do with prostitution at all but rather with granting a special favor. So-called guest prostitution was and still is practiced by many peoples (the Eskimo, Tibetans, Spartans) as a way of honoring guests.

Hospitality to guests could be extended to a legal right (based on reciprocity) that initially made possible stable trade connections between individuals and groups who were not of the same Sib.

Gift Giving

Among the Germanic peoples a gift, if it was accepted, fostered social ties. It obligated the recipient to a service in return that usually far outweighed the worth of what was received. Furthermore, the exchange of gifts gave rise to a friend relationship, which was very close to that which existed among blood relations. *The Saga of Gebe-Ref* serves as an example of this; it is a delightful inversion of the fairy-tale motif of "Hans in luck."[35] Ref is an "ash lad" whose father drives him out of the family home due to his notorious laziness. In order to be rid of the lazybones, his father gives Ref his most valuable ox. Ref then makes his luck by giving a gift at the right time and place to the right person, who in turn rewards him. First, he gives away the ox to an influential but miserly jarl. In return the stingy jarl gives him only a paltry whetstone but holds such an affection for Ref on account of the gift of the ox that he treats him like a foster son (*fóstri;* the word means both "foster son" and "foster father") and advises him to whom and in what way he should direct the whetstone and the further gifts that are exchanged for it. Ref gives away the whetstone, as his foster father advises him, and in return receives a gold ring. He gives away the gold ring, as his foster father advises him, and in return he receives a manned ship and a team of dogs. He gives away the ship and dog team, as his foster father advises him, and in return he receives personal weapons for himself. Ref gives away the weapons and in return placed at his disposal temporarily a Viking fleet. As his foster father advises him, Ref uses this fleet to extort the king's daughter, and he demands recognition as a jarl, thus becoming a made man.

If the exchange of gifts becomes professionalized and institutionalized (such as through the guest's right to hospitality), then we speak of *trade.* Active trade connections of the Germanic peoples to those of Etruscan Italy are attested from the pre-Christian era: even today the modern German word *Erz,* "ore, bronze," testifies to the trade route for raw and worked metal from the center of Etruscan metallurgy, Arēt (Aretium, present-day Arezzo), across the Alps and into Germanic territory. For the Germanic peoples knowledge of a written script also arose along a similar route, because the origins of the Germanic runes can be traced back to a North Etruscan alphabet. We can see a degenerated form of trade in the Viking practice of plundering. In its day the Viking port of Haithabu/Hedeby was an international harbor where goods were exchanged from what was then the entire known world. Further, if the geographical scope of Viking campaigns of war-for-plunder and trade is not already apparent, we can see it exemplified in a statue of the Buddha found in Sweden at Birka in Mälar Lake, another important Viking harbor.

Both of the following systems of social ties have been referred to with regard to the Vikings.

The Männerbund

A system of social ties among the Germanic peoples (and many other archaic societies) that transcended both the Sib and the various social strata was the *Männerbund* (plural *Männerbünde*).[36] This refers to a territorial coalescence of sexually mature male youths who were able to bear arms into their own cult and specific social functions. The social bonds here did not come from affiliation with a particular Sib but rather territorial affiliation with a specific gender and age group (from age twelve onward, Germanic youth were considered mature and therefore fully capable of bearing arms). Along with this came bonding through a special cult (a cultic society) with special rites of initiation. The cult god for the members of the *Männerbund* was Odin (Wotan), the god of the battle ecstasy (the "berserker rage") that the men in the cult learned to induce through certain shamanistic techniques. Because Odin was also the leader of the "Wild Army" of the dead,* in certain instances, the members of the *Männerbünde* represented the dead among the living population of the community. This touches upon a further type of bonding that came about through specific social functions. The *Männerbund* provided the elite troops for military conflicts

---

*[This Odinic "Wild Army" or "Wild Host" (*das wilde Heer* in modern German) also turns up in later European folklore. In these cases it is often referred to as the "Wild Hunt." —*Trans.*]

between (territorial) interests that transcended those of the individual Sib, and the *Männerbund* intervened in circumstances when legal mechanisms that transcended the Sib either failed or were lacking, or when familial particularism grew out of hand. The *Männerbund* was thus the upholder of censorious justice. A northern designation for a member of the *Männerbund* is *sveinn* (the source of the name Sven), which derives from the same proto-Indo-European root, *se/swe,* as does the word *Sib.* A *sveinn* was literally a young warrior among those "who belong together," which exactly fits the Sib-like (and yet Sib-transcending) bond between the members of the *Männerbund.*

In the Viking raids, which laid waste to the old world, or at least in the stereotype mentioned in the sagas of the prowling berserker bands that (in wintertime, by night[37]—the time of the raging "Wild Army") seek out isolated farms, kill the owners, and violate their wives and daughters, we can see a markedly degenerated form of *Männerbund* existence.

Männerbund-type structures continued on into the Christian era in forms such as that of the *hanse,** the guilds, sworn brotherhoods, among village and city criminals and youth gangs, and in masked societies and carnival troupes (*Narrenzünften*). The fascist movement, with its paramilitary groups (the Wehrwolf, the SA, the SS), provides examples of such degenerated forms in recent times. Further, in the political theory of National Socialism, the binding system that formed and sustained the state was considered not to be the symbiosis of man and woman in the family but rather the military association of man and man together in the *Männerbund.* In Alfred Rosenberg's view, the Prussian, and later the German, army was "one of the most grandiose examples of the architectonic [transcending of lineage and family, state-forming] *Männerbund,* built upon honor and duty and corresponding to the Nordic man."[†38]

---

*[The *hanse* were medieval trade guilds associated with the Hanseatic League in what is now northern Germany. —*Trans.*]
†Clarifications in brackets are mine.

The Retinue

The relationship of the retinue can be interpreted as an integration of the binding system of the *Männerbund* together with the binding mechanism of gift exchange, because the retinue was recruited primarily from the members of the *Männerbund* and was itself structured in a *Männerbund*-like way. What's more, it was the generosity of the king, or the lord of the retinue, that fostered and maintained the bond between him and his retainers. Thus the North and West Germanic kennings describe the king as a Breaker of Rings or Gold Diminisher (both meaning "distributor of gold"), and the Enemy of Hoards (who doesn't hoard his treasure, but spreads it to his men). Such epithets emphasized the key trait of the retinue leader, which was the decisive factor in the retinue relationship. No man was going to risk his neck for a stingy leader, and from whence should come the gifts that the men continually received from this lord (at least partially) if not "through war and plunder" (*per bella et raptus*), as the Roman historian Tacitus remarked.[39] The Vikings (Varangians) adopted the retinue as a form of social binding and organization of their raids. In turn it became the foundation for the forming of a new state (for example, Russia).

The retinue, however, could degenerate into organized terrorism, as the Dane Saxo informs us. He portrays the hustle and bustle at the court of the young king Frothi (the later lawgiver and king who reigns in peace, according to Saxo), where, as a result of a long period of military inactivity, the retinue men find their own ways to pass the time.

Some they heaved high with ropes and then pushed their dangling bodies to and fro as if they were playing at ball . . . others were stripped of their clothing and flayed with various tormenting lashes; on some they inflicted mock-hangings by fixing them with nails or in the form of a noose; some had their genitals and pubic hair scorched. Foreigners were beaten up with bones or compelled to get drunk with vast quantities of liquor till they burst. Virgins were not allowed to marry until their maidenhead had been tampered with. . . . They extended their abandoned acts of lust indiscriminately, not merely on virgins, but to a host of married women.[40]

The Cultic Society

Among its members, a cultic society fostered a Sib-transcending relationship of peace. At holy times and at holy places weapons were laid down. The inside of the temple was a "peace stead" (Old Icelandic *friðar-staðr*) where the oath ring (a ring is a symbol of binding) was kept for the ceremonial performance of oath obligations. A person who broke the sacred peace (by committing perjury or manslaughter at a holy site or on a holy occasion) became "peaceless" (Old Icelandic *frið-lauss*) and could be slain by anyone without penalty.

"In Iceland, the beginnings of state organization [that is, Sib-transcending political organization] are based upon the temple congregations," so that priests and chieftains were combined in the cultic leaders (*goðar*), "with the priesthood [the *goðar*] representing the foundation for the formation of state power."[41] The close connection between Sib-transcending cult society and the legal community found clear expression in the cultic qualification of the Thing site as a holy site (*vé*, "consecrated place, temple, cult site") and in the sacred peace of the Thing (which lasted for the duration of the Thing assembly).

Conflicts of Social Ties

Because the human being belongs to several social binding systems at the same time, it is inevitable that in certain situations conflicts will arise between these systems. Such conflicts are one of the main themes of poetry throughout the world. Here I provide two examples from the Germanic sphere.

The Germanic Sib included not only blood relatives but also those who were related by marriage. As a result, every married woman belonged simultaneously to her own Sib (via direct blood relation) and to the blood relations of her husband's Sib (via marriage). Conflicts were thus preprogrammed, especially if we take into consideration the close relationship between brother and sister among the Germanic peoples. The *Saga of the Volsungs* shows the bitter result that can come about for a married woman due to such conflicted social ties.[42] Siggeir has married Signy. At the wedding celebration he is—in his view—insulted by Sigmund, a brother of his bride. After the marriage, Siggeir gets his revenge by maliciously and gruesomely killing Signy's father and brothers when he invites them to come visit him. Only one brother, Sigmund, manages to escape. Signy, who had warned her father and brothers in vain before the attack, now secretly has a son with her brother, who must hide himself from Siggeir's pursuits. When the circumstances are right, the son shall exact blood revenge on his mother's husband. Once the son has come of age and is able to bear arms, he and Sigmund carry out the vengeance. They burn alive Siggeir and all his men in their home (*brenna inni*). Signy is offered safe passage and could save herself, but now that the revenge for her father and her brothers has been carried out upon her husband, she upholds her loyalty to Siggeir and dies alongside her spouse.

Probably the most significant Germanic literary monument that deals with a conflict of social ties between the Sib and the retinue is the *Hildebrandslied* (The Lay of Hildebrand). It was copied in the ninth century in the monastery at Fulda and is written in a mixture of Old High German, Old Saxon, and Old Low Franconian. It begins with these famous lines:

> *ik gihorta đat seggen,*
> *đat sih urhettun ænon muotin /*
> *Hiltibrant enti Hadubrant*
> *untar heriun tuem /*
> *sunufatarungo. Iro saro rihtun, /*
> *garutun se iro gudhamun,*
> *gurtun sih iro suert ana, /*
> *helidos, ubar hringa,*
> *do sie to dero hiltiu ritun.*[43]

> *I heard that said*
> *that alone strove [or met] as challengers*
> *Hildebrand and Hadubrand,*
> *from two armies, father and son.*
> *They righted their armor, donned their battle-shirts,*
> *Girded their swords,*
> *The heroes, over the (chain-mail) rings,*
> *as they rode to their (single) combat.*

Hildebrand has, together with Theodorich, fled from Odoaker (Theodorich's predecessor in Italy) to the Huns, leaving behind his wife and child. Many years later, when Theodorich's and Odoaker's armies confront one another in war, the father (Hildebrand) stands in the vanguard of the warriors on Theodorich's side, and the son (Hadubrand) stands in the vanguard on Odoaker's side. These two men are to open the battle by engaging in single combat; the outcome of their contest may even decide the greater battle. The father recognizes his son, and he attempts to make himself known and wants to give the son a gold ring. The son doesn't trust him, suspecting this to be the cowardly tricks of an "old Hun." The father can no longer avert the single combat. He cries out, *"Welaga nu, waltant got, wewurt skihit!"* ("Alas now, wielder God, a woeful fate comes to pass!"). In this single combat the father kills the son.

The same conflict of social ties that is depicted in the *Hildebrandslied* also appears in the *Shāhnāma* (The Book of Kings), the powerful epic of the Persian poet Firdausī (ca. 1000 CE). Here the Persian superhero Rustam (who is in the Iranian army) opposes in single combat his son Suhrāb (who is in the Turanian [Turkish] army). Through a sequence of events, the father and son had become separated; they have heard of one another but have never seen each other before. The son senses that he is dueling with his own father and wants to end the single combat, but he is killed by Rustam, who realizes the actual state of affairs only after it is too late.[44]

Punishments

In general, punishments[45] served to maintain the stability of the society, its values, and its systems of social ties, but we should also note that depending on the conditions, punishments could have effects in communities that were destabilizing, disintegrative (out-of-control blood revenge), or even innovative (as with the censorious justice of the *Männerbund*).

Private Punishment

Private punishment refers to a situation when the obligation to carry out the consequences for a misdeed rested either with the person affected or with his Sib. In this context we can first discuss blood revenge and then the driving out of an adulteress.

We have already seen how Germanic "familialism" exerted pressure on what might be called the "aggression threshold" of a group; an insignificant reason could cost the life of someone alien to the Sib. A few options were then available to the closest kinsman of the person killed and his Sib. These people could demand *wergeld;* if the demand was accepted and the price was received, then the matter was effectively resolved for good—or they themselves could take revenge on the killer and slay him, or they could slay any kinsman from the Sib of the killer, such as the first relative of his whom they came across, which was the more ancient possibility.[46] For the affected Sib of the first killer, either possibility presented the Sib with the same three options. If the opposing parties were unsuccessful in settling the *wergeld* demands from one another, there was triggered a chain reaction of blood revenge—one that could often continue for generations. Because the Sibs and their members, who became enemies, are intertwined with other Sibs and their members through mechanisms and systems of social ties, a snowball effect occurred: several Sibs became antagonistic to one another. Conflicts likewise arose for a Sib if it had connections to both of the warring parties. It is possible that in this situation Christianity was seen as liberation from inescapable and cataclysmic obligations.[47] We have seen that often specifically the *women* held up an example to the men and goaded them on to blood revenge.[48] The *Hávarðar saga* (Harvard's Saga, the most recent version of which dates from the fourteenth century) takes place in the tenth century and has as its main theme a man who is advanced in years and whose son is slain, but the father feels too old and weak to exact revenge. Using cleverness and cunning his wife gets him to slay the killer of his son and thus gain the admiration of all.[49]

Tacitus mentions a private punishment for adultery by a woman (the male adulterer who was involved could be slain by the husband without penalty).[50] She is dealt with by her husband. To carry out the punishment, he shears off the woman's hair, tears off her clothing, chases her from their house in plain sight of the whole Sib, and drives her out of the community with a whip. This form of punishment continued in places until the nineteenth century. Maxim Gorky describes, with utter abhorrence, having seen such a "driving out" (Russian *vývod*) in a Russian village in the province of Cherson.[51] The driving out is a "punishment of skin and hair"—in other words, a shaming punishment. At the same time, it is a "mirroring punishment," for the type of penalty somehow reflects the nature of the offense. The female's sexual power is defused by the shearing of her head, because sexual-magical power is ascribed to the woman's hair; with the disrobing she is bared;* and through the whipping she is displaced and robbed of the danger she poses to the community. In an alternative context, baring and whipping were elements of a form of fertility magic.

Public Punishment

Public punishment was that in which the punishment for a deed was carried out not at the discretion of the person affected or his Sib, but instead was dealt with by a Sib-transcending legal community or its rep-

---

*[That is to say, "exposed." —*Trans.*]

resentatives. Examples of this type of punishment included outlawry, sinking in a moor, hanging, and others.

In Iceland outlawry, or banishment (*út-legð*), was decreed by the Thing for various criminal offenses. It always also depended on how powerful the men were who brought forth a petition for the outlawing of another person and how well they could use the mechanisms and systems of social ties to the benefit of their side and against the side of the person being outlawed. Someone who killed another person in violation of an existing oath of allegiance,[52] and who was thus an oath breaker, had to have powerful protectors if he was to emerge from the situation uncondemned. Yet the oldest Icelandic legal text (dating from the twelfth and thirteenth centuries), the *Grágás*—called the "Grey Goose" because this bird was believed to attain the greatest age—makes the following determination for an oath breaker: "[t]hen shall he so far be a wolf [*vargr*], hunt and be hunted, just as far as men hunt wolves, Christians seek out churches, heathens worship shrines, fire burns, the earth becomes green, son cries for mother and mother nurses son, people light fires, a ship sails, shields flash, the sun shines . . . a Finn skis . . . the heavens revolve, the world is inhabited . . . men sow grain."[53] The "outlaw" (as the condemned man was called) became a *vargr*, a "strangler," a wolf who was hunted wherever humans live. He fell out from all systems and mechanisms of social ties: his marriage was dissolved, hospitality as a guest must be denied to him, and he could be slain by anyone without penalty. An Old English poem offers us the opportunity to sympathize with the situation in which outlawry was a catastrophe for the person affected and his family. This text is preserved for us in the Exeter Book, a codex from the eleventh century, but the poem itself may have been composed in the seventh or eighth century. In the original the poem is alliterative and divided by a refrain; it is a so-called *Frauenlied* (Woman's Song): a woman is the speaker, and the subject matter is elegiac. She laments for her beloved man who must survive far away in exile as a *wulf* ("wolf," outlaw):

For my people it is as if one brought them gifts;
will they kill [aþecgan] him, if he comes under threat?
  It's not the same for us.
Wolf is on an isle, I am on another one.
Fast is that island, surrounded by fen.
Cruel warriors are there on the island;
will they kill him, if he comes under threat?
  It's not the same for us.
For my Wolf I waited with wide-wandering thoughts,
when it was rainy weather and I sat crying.
When the battle-bold one took me in his arms
There was joy for me in that, but it was also
  loathesome.
Wolf, my wolf, the thoughts of you [wena . . . þine]
made me sick, your seldom comings,
my mourning heart—not for a lack of food.
Do you hear, Eadwacer! Our poor whelp
Wolf bears to the woods.
"One easily tears apart what was never joined"—
  our song [giedd] together.[54]

The elegy begins with a portrait of the situation, divided by a refrain, which, with antithetical images, sketches out the unequal circumstances of the female speaker and the one who is separated from her (island symbolism) and living in outlawry (or exile?). For her and her people, things are materially so good it is as if they are receiving gifts; the "wolf," by contrast, fights for pure survival among other desperados. This is followed by a flashback in the form of a love lament, apparently referring to the happy—albeit difficult—period immediately preceding the outlawry (or banishment?), a time that already cast a shadow of separation on the lovers. Then comes an accusation toward the one openly most responsible for the outlawing (or banishment?) of her beloved husband (Eadwacer, the Old English form of the Germanic personal name Odoaker) with a reference to the (small) son (the "whelp") of the separated pair, whom the father (the "wolf") apparently has taken with him into the wilderness. The ending sums up the ever-resurging pain of the separated woman in a proverblike sentence that expresses the inner circumstances the lovers both equally experience (with their unequal outer circumstances).

Alongside the rigid sentence of outlawry (peacelessness), we must consider a milder form of related punishment: banishment (expulsion from the country), either with or without a time limit. In this case the authorization to slay the offender was restricted to the territory from which the person was banished.

According to Tacitus, the Germanic peoples drowned the following groups of delinquents in bogs: *ignavos, imbelles,* and *corpore infames,* which are usually translated as "cowards," "battle-shy people," and "sexual perverts."[55] Yet what kind of specific criminal offenses these actually referred to remains unclear. The Burgundian legal text Lex Gundobada (from before 517 CE) prescribes sinking in a moor for a woman who has left her lawful husband.[56] Later this form of punishment was especially applied to women—female sexual criminals of all kinds—and it became a "mirroring elemental punishment," because bogs and swamps can be seen as chaotic degenerations of the female element of the fertile, cultivated earth. The punishment of sinking in a moor is also documented archaeologically with so-called bog corpses. The most interesting find is probably the bog corpse of Dätgen (in the district of Rendsburg, in northern Germany), which was discovered ca. 1959–1960.[57] The male corpse, which was probably sunk into a raised bog hollow in the second century CE, was naked, had its hair tied in a "Swabian knot" (a hairstyle of the freeborn), and wore a knotted strand of wool yarn around its left ankle (a magical fetter). It exhibited the following wounds and mutilations: a head that was detached, separately staked and interred; a stab wound to the chest; injuries from stabbing and beating; castration; and mutilated buttocks, which were additionally driven through with sharpened stakes. The castration may be an indication of a sexual offense. The other mutilations and the detached head, the staking, and the fetter magic with the knotted wool yarn were likely intended to hinder the deceased from any postmortem movement—that is, from returning as a destructive revenant. Bog corpse finds in areas that are now on land but were once *open* waters (flat bog finds) are, as a rule, not the corpses of those who received legal punishments but rather sacrificial victims, because certain deities were offered human sacrifices.

In the Roman period there is literary evidence for hanging as a form of public punishment. According to Tacitus, traitors and deserters were hanged on trees by the Germanic peoples.[58] The same type of death sentence was employed by the Rūs on the Volga for a robber or thief if he was caught—despite the fact that the Rūs themselves lived largely by robbery and theft. Saxo reports on the penalty decreed by Frothi, the legendary lawgiver and primordial king, for a thief and receiver of stolen goods: "A hanged thief should have a sword thrust through his sinews and a wolf fastened up at his side, so that the vicious man's likeness to the fierce animal might be demonstrated through their similar treatment."[59] Being hanged with a wolf made the criminal himself a wolf: an enemy of human society. Hanging was a "mirroring elemental punishment." It placed the thief (deserter or traitor) into the element where he belonged due to his "windy" deed and his "windy" character: the changeable, fleeting element of the turbulent air, which tosses about everything of which it catches hold. In the vengeance-oriented justice of the Third Reich, hanging again became the preferred death penalty for "traitors to the German *Volk*" (the conspirators in the July 20, 1944, plot to kill Hitler received sentences of hanging).*

Other forms of hanging that should be differentiated from its use as

---

*[This was not exclusive to Germany, however. In much of Europe as well as in the United States, hanging was long employed as a method of capital punishment, and in certain countries hanging was still seen as the traditional punishment for high treason even following World War II. —*Trans.*]

a death penalty are the hanging of a victim as a sacrifice to a deity and hanging as an initiation rite of the *Männerbund*.

We can also consider as a form of public punishment the censuring actions of the *Männerbund*. The censorious justice of the *Männerbund* could take precedence whenever Sib-transcending legal mechanisms broke down. The mode of action of the *Männerbund* members was determined by their nature as ecstatic ghostly warriors of Odin, as the initiated members of his "Wild Army" of the dead. Wherever Wotan's furious host roars forth on the night storm wind, nothing could withstand it and everything was riven by strife and swept away. Similar were the devastations ("wind punishments") left behind by the nightly censorious and penal actions of the *Männerbund* bands against those who fell out of their favor: whatever was not nailed or bolted down "ran away." Heavy objects (wagons, farm tools, etc.) turned up again in some far-off spot, such as in the airy heights atop a roof or in the crown of a tree. Houses had their roofs torn off, walls were torn down, fruit trees were cut back. Buildings were consumed by fire as if the blaze was kindled by the storm. People disappeared; they were found with their necks broken, dangling from a branch in the wind.[60] The events of the Viking Age show us that censorious justice could degenerate into terrorism, and exceptional instances of legal theft and firesetting could turn into habitual plundering and devastation.

The Rituals of Transition
(Rites of Passage)

The Germanic person did not automatically become a member of the human community (the family, the Sib) at birth and did not necessarily depart from it at death. A "ritual investment" was necessary in order to become a member of the community in the first case and to remain one in the second. Other transitional times in a person's life had to be accompanied by rites or accomplished through rites. Initiation into the *Männerbund* was ultimately a transition into a new system of social ties that granted access to a spiritual reality that was distinct from the world of normal experience. Marriage likewise signified a transition into a new system of social ties and a reception into an extended Sib network. Resettlement and land-taking represented a transition from home ground to a foreign territory, from a realm of familiar powers to one of unfamiliar or even frightening ones. This was a departure from the external conditions to which an individual was accustomed and an entrance in to a sphere of new conditions with hard-to-foresee consequences.

Birth

A newborn child did not automatically become a member of the community (family, Sib) simply through the act of birth.[1] To become a member of the community required a specific rite. The child was lifted from the ground, set on the father's knee (lap setting), and sprinkled with water (water consecration). The child received a name and, along with this "name fastening" (Old Icelandic *nafn-festr*), a gift. Water was considered an element of life; contact with water first conferred on the child life in its true sense: life in the community. A boy often received the name of his grandfather or, if his father had already died, that of his father. In any case it was thought that the deceased ancestor whose name the newborn received was reborn (Old Icelandic *endr-borinn*) in the child. A saga relates the story of a Viking who is run through by the sword of an attacker and is mortally wounded but still manages to grab hold of his opponent in such a way that he could kill him before dying from the sword wound. He lets his killer go free under the following condition: "If you or your boys are blessed with sons, do not allow my name to die out—it is from this that I hope to derive some benefit, and I want this in return for sparing your life."[2] The killer marries the slain Viking's sister, and their son receives the slain Viking's name. The essence of the deceased person, his personality, lives on in his name: the name is thus a kind of soul reincarnation. The concept of a rebirth was not at all foreign to the Germanic peoples. The modern German word for a grandson or descendant, *Enkel,* actually originally meant a "little ancestor" (compare Old High German *ano,* "ancestor"; *eninklīn,* "little ancestor"). This presumes a belief that the grandfather could be reborn as, or in, the grandson. When the father gave a gift to the new arrival at the name fastening, a gift that was likely to be an object dear to his heart, then with it he gave the newborn a piece of himself, of his soul. At this moment he enlarged the Sib, "those who belong together," with a new life. Among many archaic peoples, a gift contained some essence of the soul of the one who gave it.

As long as the ritual (lap setting, water consecration, name giving, name fastening) remained incomplete, the newborn baby could be killed by exposing it to the elements. The right to expose a child was—as we have mentioned—expressly reaffirmed when Christianity was accepted by the Icelandic Althing. Exposure was the fate of newborns who were incapable of surviving, who were sickly, crippled, or simply unwanted. It was also the fate of excess births (which were always burdened with the suspicion of "promiscuity" on the part of the mother), although, occasionally in such situations, the strongest babies were allowed to live.

If the birth ritual was completed, however, then exposure was seen as illegal. According to *Harðar saga og Hólmverja* (The Saga of Hord and the People of Holm), a late saga written in the fourteenth century, it was even considered to be murder (*þat uar mord kallath*).[3] The designation of exposure as murder in this particular case betrays the influence of Christian lawgiving, for the killing of an unbaptized child could be atoned for with money, while the killing of a baptized child was grounds for the death penalty.[4]

Initiation

The onset of sexual maturity for the male youth, and with it the ability to carry weapons, was accompanied by rites,[5] such as the ritual of admittance into the *Männerbund*. Naturally, we do not know very much about this, for such rites were a "holy mystery," which was carefully safeguarded from women and children. Through this initiation, the young man became a warrior of Odin and joined the "furious host," the "Wild Army" of the dead. The ritual consisted of mock hanging, spear marking, and (probably) tests of courage.

Through the act of spear marking (being incised with a spear, the weapon of Odin) the initiate became the property of the cultic god, and mock hanging was a technique for inducing ecstatic experiences. (Such experiences are induced in other cultures through ascetic and meditative practices, specific body postures, dance, various intoxicants, and narcotic drinks.) The prospective initiate was hoisted up by a rope around the neck until he lost consciousness, and then he was lowered again. With this, he experienced the "little death"—a new, deeper dimension of existence, transcendent existence, the spiritual reality. Odin was not only the leader of these initiated men, he was also the first initiate himself. His initiation is described in the section of the *Poetic Edda* referred to as "Odin's Rune Song."* Odin hangs himself for nine nights on the windy tree (the World Tree) wounded by a spear, sacrificed to himself, without food or drink. Screaming, he grasps downward, takes up the runes, and falls back. He drinks mead; learns magic charms; and begins to grow, thrive, and become wise in magic words and magic deeds.[6] The myth of Odin's initiation may depict the most important elements of the admittance ritual to the *Männerbund* and its effects, reduced to a human dimension.

For the young man, initiation into the *Männerbund* provided access to training in specific ecstatic techniques that enabled him to self-induce the so-called berserker rage, a battle ecstasy that created invulnerability against iron and immunity to fire and was connected to shapeshifting or soul travel. The warrior was able to transform himself into a wild animal (a bear or wolf) with the animal's aggressive traits or to separate soul forces from his body and send them out into battle in the form of an animal (bear) while his own body fell into a state of inactivity (sleep).[7]

Marriage

We are informed about the marriage ritual among the northern Germanic peoples by a comical later Eddic myth recorded in the twelfth or thirteenth century: the *Þrymskviða*. The thunder god, Thor, awakes one morning to find that he is missing his hammer—the hammer with

---

*[German translations of the *Poetic Edda* have traditionally divided the *Hávamál* into sections, with "Odin's Rune Song" being one of them. In English editions, it corresponds to stanza 111, followed by stanzas 138–45. —*Trans.*]

which he smashes the enemies of the gods and strikes lightning and rain from the clouds. The giant Thrym has stolen it, and as ransom he demands as a wife Freyja, the most beautiful of the goddesses. A trick is devised in which Thor shall travel to the homeland of the giants dressed as the bride Freyja and will then pretend to marry the giant. Because the marriage ceremony includes a hammer consecration, in which a hammer (Thor's weapon) is placed in the lap of the bride, he can thus retrieve his hammer. The divine trickster, Loki, will accompany him dressed as a maid. And so it goes. Thor gets dressed in bridal linens, and keys are hung on the bridal belt. Thus attired, he goes to the house of the giant Thrym, who can hardly wait to consummate the marriage but is quite surprised about the powerful hunger and thirst and the grimacing appearance of the "bride." Loki explains all this by saying that the bride has been unable to eat, drink, or sleep due to her lusting desire for Thrym. The giant's sister asks for arm rings from the bride, as is customary for a ceremonial gift to poor relatives. The giant calls for Thor's hammer to be brought out in order to consecrate the bride and thereby complete the betrothal before Vár, the goddess of pledges, loyalty, and love.* A split second after the bride has the hammer placed upon her knees, she lashes out with it and dispatches the giant and his clan.[8]

The important components of the marriage ritual seem here to consist of the handing over of keys, the gifts given by the bride (*brúðfé*) to the needy people in the bridegroom's clan, a hammer consecration, and the promise of mutual loyalty and love (sworn to the goddess Vár, who is the guarantor of these things). The key symbolized the wife's power over the keys of the household. Just as the wife received the keys with the act of marriage, so she had to hand them back over if she was divorced. According to Frankish legal custom, if a widow wanted to be divorced from her husband when he died, then she placed the keys on

---

*[The name Vár probably means "beloved." See the entry in Simek, *Dictionary of Northern Mythology* (Cambridge: D. S. Brewer, 1993). —*Trans.*]

the corpse or coffin of the man.[9] The hammer consecration, in which a hammer was laid on the knees of the bride, brought her loins into contact with phallic power and was intended to make them fertile, for the hammer is the weapon of Thor; he uses it to beat moisture out of the clouds and so fertilize the earth. He also uses it to kill the giants, representatives of the sterile side of nature, which is hostile to life.

Resettling and Land-Taking

The act of leaving an inhabited place, the homeland, and resettling to a new, alien place was dangerous, and for this reason, required is a ritualized operation to secure the new home.

The thirteenth-century *Laxdœla saga* (Saga of the People of Laxardale) describes the rite of a resettlement to a newly built farm. The events take place in Iceland shortly before Christianization. First, the smaller livestock leave the old farmstead. Then they are followed by the milk cow and the "money livestock" (livestock were used as a form of payment; in earlier times the Germanic word for "cattle" took on the extended meaning of "money"*). The pack animals are driven out last. The timing is arranged in such a way that at the same moment when the smaller livestock reach the new farm, the settler departs the old residence together with the pack animals. Care is taken that the marching column does not have to meander on winding paths and that there is no gap in the procession. The father of the new settler is invited to utter words of blessing as his son enters the new farm. He welcomes the new arrival, wishes him a successful existence at the new location, and predicts a long continuation of his son's name.[10] As we can see, a ritual

---

*[This relationship can be seen in the English cognate to modern German *Vieh*, "cattle," which is "fee." The Old Icelandic cognate is *fé*, "cattle, sheep, valuables, money." These Germanic words are etymologically related to Latin *pecus*, "cattle, swine, sheep" (compare English *pecuniary*, which derives from Latin *pecunia*, "property [in cattle], riches, wealth"), and similar cognates exist in other Indo-European languages. The original sense was "cattle, sheep, livestock." In a very early period this took on the related secondary sense of "wealth, possessions of value, money." —*Trans.*]

continuity is forged between the old location and the new one: as long as the chain of animals has stretched out to its full length, the departure point and destination point of the procession are magically connected to one another. In this way it is ensured that the luck or blessings of the old location carry over to the new one. Gaps in the procession or backtracking movements (winding paths) would undermine and hinder the stream of luck. A winding path would act like a magical knot that adversely hems in and "ties up" this luck. The spoken word is also present in the ritual: well wishes and a favorable prophecy will bring about that which they have proclaimed.

For the early colonists who emigrated to Iceland from Norway, the custom was reported that they took with them aboard ship the high-seat posts from their former houses. When the new country came into sight, they tossed the posts overboard. The spot where the posts floated to shore became the location for the settlement.[11]

In one instance a man took possession of land at the spot where the corpse of his father, sealed in a coffin and tossed into the water, had floated to shore. The father had not survived the sea journey, and before his death, he had ordered that this method of land-taking was to be used.[12]

The typical ritual elements for establishing a new home thus included an oracle (the landing of the high-seat posts or the coffin), luck-portending omens (the well wishes of the father; the lack of breaks and knots in the livestock procession), and a ritual management of continuity (the magical chain between the old and the new place; the old high-seat posts in the new house; the grave of the ancestor in the new ground).

Death

Once dead, people remained members of the human community if they had not already been closed off to it while alive and if they had not been denounced as enemies of the community on account of any harmful postmortem activity (as a revenant). The elaborate ritual surrounding a person's death eased the transition of the deceased into a new state of existence, staving off an overproportionate dependency of the dead upon the living and of the living on the dead in the interests of both sides and preventing harmful revenant behavior.

It was primarily the son, the heir who laid claim to the high-seat posts of the house, who also performed the "corpse rites" (Old Icelandic *ná-bjargir*) for the deceased.[13] These death rites had to be conducted from behind the corpse so that the one performing them would not fall under the gaze of the deceased, who could claim and bring him over to the side of the dead. Shutting the eyes and covering the head of the corpse was also accomplished to prevent retrieval. Washing the corpse[14] brought the dead in contact with water as an element of life and life renewal; it insured a postmortem vitality for the deceased. In order to travel to the otherworld the dead person required solid footwear, for the road to get there was long. Therefore, special *hel-skór* (Old Icelandic "Hel shoes"—that is, "shoes for Hel, the realm of the dead") were laced onto the feet of the deceased.[15] It was also important that the dead were not taken out of the house where they died through the normal doorway but rather were carried through a special opening that was broken in the wall and then sealed up again after the corpse was removed from the house. This thwarted the dead person from returning to the house, for there is a "law" governing spirits that they must always take the route they have already used.* A dead person who still harbored attachments to the living strove for close contact with the people he or she left behind, either by paying them visits (such as to sleep with a spouse)[16] or by attempting to pull over into the realm of death those who were dear to them (by fetching them into the grave).†[17] As we have seen, the

---

*Mephisto in Goethe's *Faust* comes to mind here.
†In folklore studies this is the so-called *Lenore* motif, named after Bürger's famous ballad. [Gottfried August Bürger (1747–1794) was a German Romantic poet associated with the "Göttinger Hain" (Gottingen Grove) group of *Sturm-und-Drang* writers. He is particularly noted for the creation of folk ballads such as his famous supernatural poem *Lenore*, which was published in 1773. —*Trans.*]

death ritual precluded the development of too intimate a community between the dead and the living. For this reason it was also unwise to mourn overmuch for the deceased. Mourning, it was thought, bothered the dead and prevented them from finding peace: each tear that was shed for the deceased fell, wet and cold, upon their breast, weighing them down.[18]

If the deceased person was a violent criminal while alive or someone who for other reasons (such as having died a violent or untimely death) could not be assumed to rest in peace and who had become a revenant (Old Icelandic *draugr,* a word etymologically related to modern German *trügen,* "to deceive") that endangered the living, then precautionary measures were taken against it. Heavy stones were heaped upon the corpse,*[19] and the body was driven through with stakes; it was magically fettered by winding a knotted strand of wool thread around it or by covering it with woven wickerwork[20] or thorny bushes.

We can note the burial practice employed in Greenland after Christianity and that was introduced by the Icelandic colonists. According to the thirteenth-century account in *Eiríks saga rauða* (Erik the Red's Saga),[21] people were provisionally buried in unconsecrated ground at the farm where they died, and a stake was set in their breast. Later, when the weather conditions allowed for the arrival of the priest, the stake was pulled out and holy water was poured into the opening. Then the corpses were brought to the nearest church, and "the priests sang prayers over them" (held a mass for the dead). They were then buried there permanently in consecrated ground. As long as the dead remained in unconsecrated soil, they were considered potential revenants, and they were fixed in the ground with a stake. Once they had been transferred to the churchyard and were integrated into the Communion of the Saints according to Christian ritual, they rested and no longer posed a threat to the living.

To one degree or another, rituals that accompanied the death of

---

*The female bog corpse found at Windeby in northern Germany was held down with a stone.

a human being presupposed—and were more or less closely associated with—definite conceptions about the fate of a person after death. This might then be the appropriate place for a brief account of the so-called eschatology of the individual, as scholars of religion call it. As a preface we should note that such conceptions could be locally delimited or may have related only to certain strata of society. They could have formed a part of general folklore, or perhaps they were poetic literary constructions. They may even have been learned or ironic systematizations (with a Christian influence). Sometimes they were several of these things all at once.

Life after Death

Both within the Germanic realm and well beyond it there is evidence for the conception that a dead person could continue to exist in the grave (as well as outside of it) as a "living corpse."[22] At burial the corpse was therefore outfitted with everything that was cherished and necessary during the person's life. People possessed of a special "sight" were able see the dead in their grave mounds and to hear them singing; the light that illuminated the mound cast no shadows (just as the dead themselves generally cast no shadows).[23] From the burial site a deceased person often exhibited activity as a revenant, which was dangerous to the living. An animated corpse's appearance was similar to that of a living person, only its energies were amplified into the monstrous. A dead person could also shapeshift (for instance, into the form of an animal). The manner in which the living dead were able to change their location (via sudden disappearance and appearance) was paranormal. A revenant could be dispersed by burning its body on a pyre.[24]

The idea that the deceased person lived on in the grave mound had a parallel in the belief that the dead continued to live on in specific mountains (the grave mound is an artificial, stylized mountain).[25] It was said of the chieftain and colonist Thorolf that at the location of his land-taking in Iceland he worshipped a stony mound, which he called a holy mountain, and he believed that he would enter into this mound when he died, as would all of his kinsmen.[26] The legends of dead hero-emperors who live on inside certain mountains (Barbarossa in the Kyffhäuser mountain, Charlemagne in the Odenberg or the Untersberg) attest that the belief regarding the mountain as a residence for the dead was also present in the southern Germanic realm.*[27]

The northern Germanic peoples recognized a kingdom of the dead that existed at the bottom of the sea and which was under the dominion of the sea goddess Rán. The southern and eastern Germanic peoples assumed that the souls of the dead returned to certain sacred lakes from which they were incorporated into new human beings. This is strongly suggested at least by the derivation of the word *soul* (from proto-Germanic *saiwa-lō,* "belonging to the lake, deriving from the lake") from a term for "lake," or "inland sea" (*saiwaz*),† together with the fact that the word *soul* is indigenous only to the South and East Germanic linguistic areas, whereas in the north there were originally other designations for it. The German term *Kinderteich* (children's pond) and the stork that delivers babies are motifs from this conceptual sphere.‡[28] They attest to a common belief, also held by the North Germanic peoples, that the dead were reborn in certain human beings. Among the Germanic coastal dwellers, the ritual of ship burial corresponded to the myth of a kingdom of the dead beyond the sea.[29]

The northern, southern, and eastern Germanic peoples all recognized an underworld kingdom of the dead called, in Old Norse, Hel

---

*Hitler, with his "weakness" for the cult of the dead, could gaze out onto the Untersberg mountain from his Berghof residence and thus felt himself strengthened in his "summoning."

†[Proto-Germanic *saiwaz* is the source for our English word *sea* and the modern German *See*, "lake." The sense here is of a landlocked body of water rather than the open ocean; compare usages such as the Baltic Sea, the Black Sea, and so forth. —*Trans.*]

‡[Common motifs in regional German folklore are that of the *Kinderteich*, "children's pond," and *Kinderbrunnen*, "children's well," and the like: a small body of water or spring that is said to bring forth children. —*Trans.*]

("the hidden," "the veiled," "the concealing"), which was also personified as a goddess of the same name. Due to Christian influence at a very early stage, the corresponding word among the eastern and southern Germanic peoples came to designate the horrible underworldly site of punishment for the damned, and from this we get our modern sense of hell. (According to the older Germanic understanding, Hel was not a place of punishment.)

The North Germanic sources offer detailed depictions of the heavenly places where the dead reside.[30] First, there is Odin's Valhalla (Old Icelandic Val-hǫll, the "hall" of those who have fallen on the battlefield) in heavenly Asgard (Ásgarðr), the realm of the Ases (a specific class of gods). The inhabitants of Valhalla, the heroes who died in battle, amuse themselves by engaging in single combat (this is the source of their name, *einherjar*, "single warriors"). They died as a result, only to be resurrected (unwounded) again. They drink beer from the ever-full udders of the goat Heidrun (literally, "she who is possessed of a shining secret"—or just mead?) and are served at their banquets by the Valkyries (literally, "the choosers of the slain on the battlefield"). Through their initiation, the young members of the *Männerbund* are also counted among the heavenly ghost warriors of Odin (the *einherjar*); their ecstatic actions are reflected in the myth of Wotan's "Wild Army." Another otherworldly location for the dead is Folkvang (*Fólk-vangr*, "meadow of the folk"), the residence of the goddess Freyja. Because the word *vangr* refers to a "green field" or "meadow" (compare the Alemannic topographical names *Wangen, -wangen*), we are tempted to think of the green paradise mentioned in the account of the Rūs.

The dead were also believed to be (simultaneously) localized in more than one place, for example, both in Valhalla and as living corpses in grave mounds. The Eddic story of the night of love between Sigrun and the dead Helgi offers poetic evidence for this belief.*[31] These sorts of thoughts are not unfamiliar to us modern people when we think, for

---

*Helgi is simultaneously an enraptured inhabitant of Valhalla and Sigrun's (his widow's) "accessible" lover in the (opened) grave mound.

instance, that our deceased loved ones are simultaneously "in heaven," "at the cemetery," and somehow "around us" as well.

A dead person could die again—and indeed once and for all. This "second death," or "redeath," was undergone by revenants when they were destroyed in order to free the living from their harmful activities. (They killed humans and livestock, harried whole tracts of land, and rode at night on the ridges of rooftops.) The second death was inflicted when the body of the living corpse was maimed in such a way that it halted any ability for further movement. This was done by beheading the corpse and burying it either with the head between its legs or else separately (an inverted juxtaposition or a separate head burial). This second death could be accomplished even more securely by burning the living corpse and strewing the ashes in the ocean or covering them in a deserted place, far away from human beings.[32]

For the Germanic peoples, as for many other cultures, the postmortem wandering of a revenant is not a direct consequence of the moral-religious behavior of the person during his or her lifetime (in contrast, for example, to the idea that appropriate penance for actions in this world will be made in the next, as is central to Christianity).[33] There are quite a few other factors that determined a person's otherworldly existence: the mode of death, social status, and gender. A man who dies in battle goes to Odin in Valhalla or to Freyja's Folkvang; someone who drowns in the sea goes to Rán's watery kingdom; someone who dies of old age or disease goes to Hel. The nobleman goes to Odin and the peasant to Thor, for if they follow their divine patron voluntarily into death, then they would remain together with him. Women go to Hel, while virgins (but apparently also some married women[34]) go to Freyja. Postmortem conditions for the dead also depend on the material provisions accorded to them by the living. The time and manner in which a person is reborn depend on whether someone, and which person, bears the name of the deceased. A person who was a violent criminal and a miscreant in life continued after death as a monstrous revenant and living corpse if the living themselves were not able to take radical action to prevent it. The Eddic literature mentions an otherworldly place of punishment called Nástrǫnd ("corpse strand, corpse beach")—a place for oath breakers, murderers, and adulterers. It is depicted as a landscape formed from snakes and sprinkled with poison, and its inhabitants wade in the currents of a poisonous swamp where a wolf and a dragon tear at their dead flesh. But in light of the fact that Odin, the father of the gods himself, commits oath breaking, murder, and adultery, the formulation of Nástrǫnd may well be due to Christian influence.*

---

*Completely un-Germanic is the particular reference in relation to Nástrǫnd that describes adultery as the *husband's* treachery as opposed to that of the wife.

Magic

Along with the times of transition that occur in the life of a human being, there are other critical situations that necessitate a ritual effort—for example, to insure protection against an extraordinary threat or to exert extraordinary influence upon other people. In contrast to rites of passage, we call this kind of ritual effort sorcery or magic. The modern German word for "magic" is *Zauber,* from Old High German *zoubar.* The original meaning of the German word *Zauber* can still be discerned from its Old English cognate, *tēafor,* which designated "red coloring, ochre, red chalk," or "ointment." This points to the practice of staining runes that have been carved for magical ends with blood or some red substance (ersatz blood) in order to properly make the rune magic effective. Socially speaking there is a distinction between permissible, or white, magic (Old Icelandic *galdr,* "screaming, incantatory magic, sorcery"), and impermissible, or black, magic (Old Icelandic *gandr,* "magic stave, sorcery, witchcraft"; or *seiðr,* "cord, fetter, sorcery"). In impermissible magic the ritual effort is ultimately aimed at the malicious harming of another person. I will not draw a fundamental distinction between sorcery and magic. Those who wish to distinguish the two might regard magic as a specific technology of which sorcery (but also any other ritual) avails itself. Here I present the following categories: incantatory magic, rune magic, death magic, divinatory magic, cursing magic, and destructive magic. Cursing magic and destructive magic are categorized as impermissible sorcery (black magic). The other types fall into this category only when they are employed for malicious ends. At the time of Tacitus (ca. 100 CE) women were considered by the Germanic peoples to be especially talented in magic.[1]

Incantatory Magic

A fundamental assumption of magic is that the spoken word itself has innate power to "evoke"* and produce what it expresses. Exactly for this reason the *correct* word must be uttered. (A slip of the tongue ruins a magical effect or directs the effect back against the one who has misspoken.) Formulaic types of speech and singing strengthen the magical power of the word.

This example of incantatory magic comes from an eleventh-century Old English manuscript. The charm itself may be considerably older—certainly the underlying ideas are, for they reach back to heathen prehistory.

> *Here he came in, in spider shape,*
> *he had his garments [*hama; *compare modern German*
>   Hemd, *"shirt"] in hand.*
> *He said that you shall be his steed,*
> *he laid his reins around your neck.*
> *They began to alight from the land.*
> *As soon as they left from land,*
> *then they began to cool down, though.*
> *Then the sister of the beast came in.*
> *Then she put an end to it, and swore oaths:*

---

*[This word is very descriptive and literally appropriate here: its etymology is from Latin *ex-vocare,* "to call out or call forth." —*Trans.*]

That this should never hurt the sick man,
*nor him who could obtain this charm [*galdor*],*
*nor him who knew how to chant [*on-galan*] this*
charm.[2]

The charm protects against what in German folklore is called a
Mahrtenritt (an attack by a nightmare demon that descends upon and
"rides" the sleeping victim). Throughout the Germanic realm, there was
a widely known belief that sorcerers and sorceresses could send soul
forces out of their body or could alter their form and slip through key-
holes or cracks in the door and into the bedrooms to torment people
in their sleep. Such nightmare demons could, for instance, transform
sleeping people into horses by putting halters on their victims, sitting on
them, and riding them for the entire night until they were completely
exhausted. The sleeper who was thus befallen experienced the sorcerous
force as a nightmare and as a demonic attack, and, if it was repeated, felt
a weakening loss of strength or an illness.[3] This charm records in words
how a nightmare demon is caught in the act and banished. Having
transformed himself into the shape of a spider, the demon gains access
(through a small crack in the wall or in a closed door) to the sleeping
place of his victim. He carries his regular clothing in his hand (for if he
should lose it or someone should rob him of it, he would lose the ability
to return to his normal form). By using a charm and putting reins on
the victim he turns the victim into his "steed" and begins to ride (with
the journey proceeding through the air). The magically adept sister of
the ridden victim (the "beast") then stealthily enters and brings an end
to the demon by "forswearing" him. What was successful in the past
(the charm is kept in the past tense of "mythic precedence") must also
work in the present.

With its repetitive speech, the recitation of the charm during a current emergency deploys the power that had been efficacious in the past.
One of the prefatory instructions for using the charm (not reproduced
here) recommends singing (*singan*) the charm into both ears and then

above the head of the person afflicted. The charm should also be written and fastened in the form of an amulet around the recipient's neck by a young girl (who here ritually represents the mythical "sister"). The act of writing the charm strengthens the magic by making it permanently fixed and available. In this way verbal magic becomes written magic.

Rune Magic

The written word is more effective than the spoken one. It does not need to be continually repeated, because it "stands as written." It is, nevertheless, also more susceptible to contingencies: the written charm can be erased or scraped off (by the person for whom it is intended or by another person), thus depriving it of its magical power. To prevent it from being read and understood (by the wrong recipient) and thus rendered ineffective, the author of the charm may have to encipher it—that is, arrange initial letters to stand for a word (creating an acrostic) or scramble the letters of a word (creating an anagram) or arrange them in such a way that only the *author* knows its true meaning (and magical effect), while the charm is inacessible to those for whom it is not intended.[4] As the color of life, red confers the letters—and thus the written word—with heightened magical power.

Rune magic is written magic, and it operates according to the laws that govern written magic. The Germanic runic script may have been derived from a North Etruscan alphabet. If the engravings on the Meldorf brooch (found in the region of southern Ditmarsch) are in fact runes (reading: *hiwi* and presumably meaning "for Hiwi," with Hiwi being a personal name), they would lend support to the hypothesis that suggests the runes were developed in the second century BCE.[5] If this is the case then the oldest description of rune magic would have been provided by Tacitus. He comments that to discern the future the Germanic peoples made use of a lot-casting oracle. They cut small wooden staves from a fruit-bearing tree (a dead tree would spell disaster), marked them with various signs (*notae;* here probably meaning "runes"), and cast them onto a cloth, letting them fall as fate decreed. The person conducting the divination rite picked up three staves, one after the other, and interpreted the outcome according to the incised signs (runes).[6] So, for example, a ↑-rune on a stave that was picked up would have acrostically referred to the god of the legal assembly and of war, Tīwaz, and thus to coming war and victory. The same oracular practice is later attested in literary evidence from the northern Germanic peoples. A vestige of this practice lingers on in the German expression *Buchstaben lesen* (that is, "to read letters"), which actually means "to gather up beech staves (incised with runes)," and, by doing so, to gather something from them about the future.

The pattern of recurring runic formulas in the northern Germanic realm includes the words *alu* and *laukaR*, either alone or combined with other words. Alongside complete pieces of text are also found acrostic abbreviations using *Begriffsrunen* (single runes that stand in for an entire word, such as *l* for *laukaR*) or anagrammatic distortions (such as *lua* for *alu*), by means of which counter magic is hindered or made impossible. Of great interest is the arrival of metal bracteates in the fifth and sixth century CE. These decorative coins of gold were worn as medallions or amulets. The word *laukaR* means "leek." In magical praxis leeks (or garlic or onions) were considered antidemonic substances believed to have antiseptic and aphrodisiacal powers.* Wearing a bracteate on the chest with the runic inscription "leek" guaranteed the wearer the continuing effective power of the leek, without necessitating the possession and use of the plant itself (and without the immediate nuisance of its smell!). The meaning of *alu* is debated, but it was probably related to notions of aid, strengthening, and protection (akin to the Old Icelandic verb *ala*, "to make big, to nourish," and related to German *alt* and English *old*, meaning "grown").[7] The rune formula *alu* then grants the wearer of a bracteate (male or female) a written magical aid and protection in any situation.[8]

---

*Similar effects are ascribed to flax (linen) (see the reference to the *lina laukaR* inscription on pp. 3–4). Moreover, compare the Old Icelandic kennings for "woman," such as Linen Goddess and Linden of the Leek, among others.

Further varieties of rune magic are utilized for death magic, cursing magic, and destructive magic and will be presented in those particular sections.

Death Magic

Death magic concerns *necromancy:* the conjuration of the dead whose help a person wishes to secure. Death signifies an increase in power, and this power can be put to use by the living. Death magic is seen as permissible when the living people who engage in it are the children of the deceased; if they are strangers, then such death magic is considered to have a black magical intent.

In the north the magic charm (*val-galdr,* a "death charm" or "death song") for summoning a dead person from the grave (the underworld) is a "waking song,"[9] because it began with the formulaic wake-up call *"Vaki!"* ("Awake!"). Hervor, a young Viking maiden, "wakes" her dead father, Angantyr, in order to obtain his magic sword from the grave mound: *Vaki, Angantýr! Vekr þik Hervǫr!* . . . ("Awake, Angantyr! Hervor wakes you! . . ."),[*10] and Svipdag, who has a spell cast upon him by his evil stepmother (because he spurned her erotic advances), wakes his proper mother, Groa, from the realm of the dead at the grave mound and appeals to her for help: *Vaki, þú, Groa! Vaki þú, góð kona!* ("Awake, Groa! Awake, you good woman!")[11†]

When someone wakes a dead person who is not a family relation with the aim of obtaining information about the future, the prophecy thus coerced could turn out to be a curse: the dead person announces

---

*[This poem is typically referred to in English as "The Waking of Angantyr." For the complete translation, see Patricia Terry, trans., *Poems of the Elder Edda,* revised edition (Philadelphia: University of Pennsylvania Press, 1990), 248–53. I have translated the line above more literally, in line with both Hasenfratz's original text and the death charm formula under discussion here. —*Trans.*]

†[This poem forms the first part of the Eddic poem referred to as *Svipdagsmál.* For an English translation, see Henry Adams Bellows, trans., *The Poetic Edda* (New York: American-Scandinavian Foundation, 1923), 234–51. —*Trans.*]

the waker's doom. According to Saxo, this is what happens to a magical female giant who, together with her human partner, forces a corpse to speak by placing under its tongue a little wooden stave that she has carved with "a horrible rune song" (*dira carmina*). The dead person's words predict the giant's immanent death—and prove terrifyingly true.[12]

The earliest evidence for death magic in the north may be a bracteate with anagrammatically rearranged Latin letters, which are sequenced to read the same in both directions. They are assumed to be an encipherment of the word *sisu* (meaning some kind of death magic). The bracteate was discovered inside the mouth of a corpse in a southern Swedish grave.[13] By means of written magic, the living apparently wanted to insure the availability of the deceased for counsel and assistance (or they may have desired to protect the deceased from the death magic of others). Death magic was naturally practiced in the South Germanic realm as well. The *Indiculus Superstitionum et Paganiarum,* a church index of "superstitions and heathen customs" from the period and geographical area in which Bonifatius was active, refers in its second section to a "sacrilege committed over the dead" (*sacrilegium super defunctos*) and includes the heathen name for it: *dadsisas*.[14] We can easily see the similarity between the second component in this term, *-sisas,* and the word on the bracteate medallion (*sisu*), and between the first component, *dad-,* and our word *dead*. The heathen sacrilege over the graves of the deceased would have thus been death magic, the conjuration of the dead.

Divinatory Magic

In the north there were wandering seeresses. The designation for such a seeress was *vǫlva,* a "female bearing a staff." (Compare *vǫlr* "staff.") If people desired to find out about the future, they invited one of these seeresses as a guest and provided hospitality to her. In saga literature there is a detailed (or fanciful?) description of a seeress and her activities. She wears a blue cloak (like the magically adept Odin) and clothing made of animal fur, and in her hand she wields a staff (a magical staff, whence her name). She partakes of a special diet, eating, for her meat, only animal hearts. (The heart, as the seat of life, guarantees an optimal supply of power.) To conduct her divination, she sits elevated on a magical seat, the *seið-hjallr* (magic platform). The women who are present form a magical protective circle around the platform. Special magical singing apparently puts her into a kind of shamanistic trance. Also suggestive of a shamanistic trance is the remark that, before her divination, the seeress opens her jaws and yawns. Apparently, gold given to her at the right moment could alter the divination for whoever makes the donation.[15]

Other forms of divination, such as the rune oracle and the black magic variety of necromancy, have already been discussed.

Cursing Magic

In the north, the performance of an act of cursing magic proceeded like so: a horse is slaughtered and its head is cut off and stuck on a pole, which is then declared a *niðstǫng* (a "scorn pole"; Old Icelandic *nið* is cognate to modern German *Neid*, "envy, jealousy," but it originally meant "hatred, scorn, aggression"). The *niðstǫng* is erected so that the horse's head gazes in the direction of the place where the scorned person lives or toward a spot where the scorned person will have to pass and thus fall under the gaze of the horse's head. The erection of a *niðstǫng* can be accompanied by spoken and runic magic (a charm is uttered aloud and the corresponding runes are carved into the wooden pole), which strengthens the effect of the magic. On the other hand, if the person for whom it is intended sets eyes on the *niðstǫng*, he or she can "reverse" the magic (by uttering an appropriate charm) so that it does not affect him or her, but instead *backfires* on the person who cast the scornful curse.[16]

The erection of the head on a pole is related to the practice of horse sacrifice (the preeminent and most effective animal sacrifice to the deity). Through the sacrificial act, the sacrificed animal becomes the property of the god and is magically engaged with the divine sphere of power; the parts of the sacrificed animal—especially the head—retain the power to banish and repel what is counter to the divine.[17] The person at whom the impaled horse head is directed is thus branded *by name* (for repulsion) as the enemy of the gods and humans, and therefore of the community. That person becomes a *niðingr* (another word for *vargr,* "criminal," "wolf"),* is banished, and becomes an outlaw. Cursing magic is seen as a form of black magic, for the outlawing of a person can be decreed only by the legal community or its representatives—and not by any private individual on the basis of a personal whim.

Even today, the decorative horse heads found on the gables of German farmhouses recall their former apotropaic (evil-dispelling) function. In the place of the horse head on the gable, a horseshoe over the door serves just as well.

Destructive Magic

We have already encountered some destructive magical practices in our discussions of death magic and curses. The type of destructive magic that we will now consider is aimed at the physical annihilation of another human being. Here is an example from northern Germanic territory.

In the *Grettis saga* (Grettir's Saga), written in the fourteenth century, it is told that the tenth-century Icelandic saga hero Grettir is "finished off" by his adversaries through destructive magic when no other method is available.[18] The sorcerous foster mother of one of his enemies carves runes in a dead tree trunk, reddens them with her blood, then walks backward and widdershins (leftward is the direction of death) around the trunk, all the while muttering incantatory charms (*galdr*).

---

*[*Niðingr* might be literally translated as "despised person," or, in this case, "accursed person." —*Trans.*]

When Grettir later tries to split the tree trunk with an ax, the edge of the tool bounces off the wood and lands in his upper thigh, thus inflicting the wound that leads to his death.

Magic in *Burchard's Corrector*

In Book 19 of his collection of church decrees, Bishop Burchard of Worms (d. 1025) provides a penitential and confessional book (known as the *Deutsches Bußbuch,* or *Burchard's Corrector*)[19] that relates the confessional practices employed by the German church among the populace. The confessional questions in the text address specific acts that the church disapproved of and for which corresponding church penances were imposed. Those of interest here are the questions that refer to sorcery. They reflect traditional (heathen) magical practices in the South Germanic realm—although, while we examine them, we should note that magic is a cross-cultural phenomenon, and we can therefore speak of a "koine of magic."* Here, we look at some examples (couched in the terms of confessional questions) of destructive magic and, as new topics to consider, of love magic and rain magic.[20]

Love Magic

> Do you do what certain women are in the habit of doing? They take their menstrual blood and mix it into food or drink and give it to their husbands to eat or to drink, so that they will be more lusted after by them. If you have done that. . . . [This is followed by a church penance.]

Commentary: Blood is considered a "soul substance." If a person mixes his or her blood with that of another person, or ingests someone else's blood, they are magically bound to the other. If the blood in question

---

*[In other words, although the details may vary according to the specific cultural context, magical practices also exhibit similar traits, cross-culturally. —*Trans.*]

comes from a sexual area of the body, this determines the type of bond sought. This form of love magic was widely known throughout the Germanic sphere and is in no way relegated to the distant past.

> Do you do what certain women are in the habit of doing? They lie face down, expose their hindquarters, and have bread prepared on top of their naked bottom, which, when baked, is given to their husbands to eat. They do this so that they [their husbands] fall more ardently in love with them. If you have done this. . . . [This is followed by a church penance.]

Commentary: A person who ingests something that has come into magically directed contact with the (naked) body of another person is then magically bound to that person (through contact magic). Again, the place of contact (an erogenous zone) determines the type of bond (sexual love). Additionally, the bread eaten by the "victim" represents the body of the sorceress (analogous magic)—and the "victim" himself incorporates, in the true sense of the word, the "victimizer": he will enjoy "feasting" on her from that point on. The position of the belly (with the body exposed) of the woman engaged in the sorcery corresponds to the altar position of the woman in a Black Mass.

Destructive Magic

> Do you do what certain woman are in the habit of doing? They take their clothes off and spread honey all over their naked body. Thus smeared with honey, they roll frequently to and fro on the floor on top of a linen cloth that is strewn with grains of wheat. They carefully pick off all the wheat clinging to their wet body and put it into the mill and grind it into flour by making the mill go backwards, against the course of the sun (*retrorsum contra solem*).* From this

---

*[That is, widdershins. —*Trans.*]

flour they make bread and give it to their husbands to eat so that when they have eaten it they become feeble and waste away. If you have done this. . . . [This is followed by a church penance.]

Commentary: In terms of its magical structure, this example of destructive death magic is like an inverted form of love magic. By milling the flour leftward the mill is turned in the direction of death, and the flour and honey becomes a kind of deadly food instead of a source of love and vitality. Whoever consumes bread prepared in such a manner will waste away and die.

Do you believe what many women believe and hold true, women who have reverted to Satan? Namely that in the silence of restless nights,[21] although you lie in bed and your man is asleep at your bosom while you are physically behind closed doors, you are able to depart and cross the spaces of the world with others laboring in the same deluded state, and with invisible weapons slay baptized Christians who are redeemed through the blood of Christ, boil their flesh and consume it, and stuff straw or wood or other things in the place where their heart was, and reanimate those you have eaten and extend their lease on life. If you have believed this. . . . [This is followed by a church penance.]

Commentary: In earlier discussions of the "berserker procession" and the nightmare demon, we have seen that soul travel and shapeshifting were two experiential and descriptive variants of the same type of phenomenon. The ability magically to shapeshift was also ascribed to the witch, as was the ability to disengage her soul from her body and (while her body was in a state of immobility) to let it roam. This latter ability is described here. The belief that witches (either in a transformed state or while outside of their bodies) could cut out the organs from the chests of their nighttime victims and stuff the holes with straw or some other substance (with the result that the magically mutilated person would suddenly die at a specific time) is attested all the way back to antiquity, as well as among the northern Germanic peoples.[22]

Weather Magic

> Do you do what certain women are in the habit of doing? If they need rain and have none, they gather several young girls and choose one to be the leader who is definitely a virgin. They strip her and lead the naked girl out of the village to a place where they find Hyoscyamus [Henbane], which in German is called Belisa. They have her dig up this plant with the little finger of the right hand and they fasten the uprooted plant to the little toe of the right foot with a string. Then the girls, each of whom holds a twig in her hands, lead the virgin, who is dragging the plant behind her to the nearest river, and with these twigs, they sprinkle the virgin with river water, thus hoping with their sorceries [or magic songs?—the original text reads *incantationes*] to make rain. Then they lead the aforementioned virgin naked, as she is, and with her footsteps being transposed in the manner of a crab, on her hands away from the river and back to the village. If you have done that, or consented to. . . . [This is followed by a church penance.]

Commentary: This text may be the oldest evidence for the so-called Rain Maiden. (Even today in the Balkan countries during an incessant drought, a naked girl is bedecked with green leaves, and water is poured over her.) In the rite described the naked virgin with the henbane plant (henbane functions as a magical drug: its ingestion produces auditory hallucinations that are akin to the sound of rain)[23] tied to her represented the plant-bearing earth that, in order to become "bearing," must have been fertilized by the (male) heavens. The event of fertilization (by rain) was imitated (imitational magic) by sprinkling the river water with twigs (the ceremonial "rod of life" as a phallic symbol*). If the virgin "turned her back on" or "gave a cold shoulder" to the water the entire effort would be for naught: by turning away, she would set the magic into reverse. This is also the reason for her "crab walk." The digging up and fastening of the henbane to the right side was probably due to that side being the "side of life"—as opposed to left, the "side of death." A magical charm (*incantationes*) that might have been similar to the one sung to the German girl during the rite of sprinkling, or fertilizing, the rain maiden (earth) has been preserved for us in Old English.

> *Erce, Erce, Erce, mother earth [eorðan modor]!*
> *Hallowed be you, field, mother of men!*
> *May you be growing in the embrace of [the] God [of*
>   *heaven],*
> *filled with food, to the benefit of men!*[†24]

Like our word *earth*, Erce is probably a formation from the root *er-*, meaning "earth." (Compare also the Old High German word *ero*, "earth.")[‡]

---

*[Hasenfratz uses the German folkloric term *Lebensrute*, which literally translates to "rod of life." In English folklore studies, the term usually appears in its German form or sometimes with this translation. In many seasonal folk customs (such as Fasching and Carnival parades, midwinter processions, and wassailing ceremonies) switches or whips made from green twigs or bundles of twigs are used symbolically to promote fertility and new life by swatting at women's bottoms or by striking against a tree. The term *Lebensrute* generically refers to any implement of this type. —*Trans.*]

†Translation (and expansions in brackets) mine.

‡[In the original text Hasenfratz draws the etymological parallel to modern German *Erde*, a word that is cognate to English *earth* and identical in meaning. —*Trans.*]

The Powers

The religious human being finds himself or herself confronted with a multitude of powers, which are often experienced as individual entities embodied in a particular form. These powers include the human being and whatever manifests itself to him or her, the supernatural beings that make up so-called lower mythology, the deities, and the powers of fate (or fate itself).

The Human Being

A human being is experienced as a power, and power reveals itself to the human being.[1] We have seen how in certain respects a dead person as compared to a living person experienced an increase in power. The dead person possessed knowledge of the future, which the living (using death magic) could gain access to and utilize. The living corpse, and the revenant in particular, has command of monstrous physical forces. A revenant could shift its physical location in a way that a living person could not, and it also had the ability to transform its shape.

We have seen how living people could send psychic forces (the so-called *Exkursionsseele*, or "traveling soul") out of the body, which then collapsed in immobility, and were able to harm the bodies and lives of their fellow human beings in a cannibalistic way (such as in night travels by witches). We have seen how someone could gain access to sleeping people in an altered form (for instance, as a spider), in order to torture his or her victims as a night demon (the *Mahrtenritt*), and we have seen how the elite warriors of the *Männerbund* self-induced the supernatural energies of wild bears or wolves (taking on their forms),[2] or were able to release the traveling soul from their body in the shape of an animal and send it into battle. One facet of this phenomenon was the werewolf, feared throughout the entire Germanic realm and beyond: a man (Old High German and Old English *wer*, "man"; compare the term *wer-geld*) who was able to transform himself at will into a ravenous wolf.[3] The modern German word *Geist* (which means "mind" or "spirit") originally referred to a traveling soul that a sorcerer or sorceress dispatched from his or her body in the form of a "frightful spook with which to torment others."* In the southern Germanic realm, therefore, the response to the third article in the Christian confession was a source of potential trouble, because to the ears of the early Christians, the declaration *"Ich glaube an den heiligen Geist"* may have sounded like "I believe in the Holy Spook"! It was preferable to confess: "I believe in the Holy Spirit (*atum wihan*)."

Although earlier we saw that the body of the "sender" collapsed into immobility (sleep, stasis) while the traveling soul was engaged in activities, there was an exception to this rule. If those in an active waking state encounter their own traveling soul, this is taken to be a premonition of death: the person is seeing their soul as it is about to leave his or her body. In the north, this soul appears in the form of a woman (*fylgju-kona*, a "woman who follows," because she is normally an invisible companion of the living person). Elsewhere, she appears as a doppelgänger (in which case the person encounters his or her own exact likeness and realizes he or she does not have long to live).

---

*[The English word *ghost*, which is directly cognate to German *Geist*, still overtly represents the older sense of meaning to which Hasenfratz refers. —*Trans.*]

First, we can consider the story of Bödvar Bjarki (the last name means "little bear"). During the decisive battle between Hrolf, king of the Danes, and his brother-in-law (who is attempting to seize the crown), next to the king appears a powerful bear, an animal that decimates everything in its path and proves itself to be invulnerable. At the same time, the king's bravest fighter, Bödvar Bjarki, has disappeared. He is found sitting in the hall, groggy and sleepy, far from the tumult of the battlefield, and is urged to go into combat. Although resistant at first, he does so, but states that in many respects he will be of much less use to his king than he was before he was disturbed. This is true: as soon as Bödvar strides next to the king, the raging bear is gone; the tide of victory shifts definitively to the opposing side.

Second, we must consider the story of the Icelander Thorgils. He rides with his men in the summer to the assembly, the Thing. As he nears the assembly plain, he and his retinue see a large woman screaming at them from the Thing site. Thorgils rides up to her, but she dodges around him. It is his *fylgja*. Soon afterward, Thorgils is slain by an ax blow in the back from a jealous aggressor.

Supernatural Beings of Lower Mythology

The supernatural beings of lower mythology[4] are those creatures that we find in Germanic folktales and fairy tales: giants, dwarves, wights, elves (hidden people), nixies, and so forth,[5] which J. R. R. Tolkien poetically gives new life to in his books *The Hobbit, The Lord of the Rings,* and *The Silmarillion.* These creatures are thought to be closer to human beings than the Germanic gods in that they can associate with humans through persistent connections similar to marriage (such as the so-called *Mahrtenehe**). Gods, too, can enter into relationships with humans (and

---

*[The *Mahrtenehe* refers to the legendary motif of a marriage between a *Mahrte,* a female supernatural being, and a mortal male. The word *Mahrte* is cognate to archaic English *mare,* a term that persists in the second part of our compound word *nightmare*). —*Trans.*]

humans can descend from gods), but such unions are not lasting, except for the case in which a temple priestess is seen as the wife of the god whom she serves.

Here are the designations for these types of beings as they appear in the Old Icelandic sources.[6]

Giants had various names: *jǫtunn* (from *etunaʀ*, "eater"), *þurs* (probably related to Old Indic *turá*, "strong"), or *troll* (which can probably be connected to Middle High German *trüllen*, "to entertain, to beguile"). They are representatives of the infertile, rocky, icy, and hostile aspects of the natural world, which continually threaten the places inhabited by humans and gods. They especially have it in for Freyja, the goddess of fertility and love. Thor, who pounds out fertilizing moisture from the clouds with his lightning hammer, is their most bitter opponent. The giants existed before the gods, who (matrilineally) descended from them. Giantess maidens are in demand as erotic playthings by the male gods; they are also not spurned as spouses. On the other hand, giants can abduct human women, and giants' daughters can fall in love with human warriors. If giants are caught off-guard by the rising sun when they are out on their nightly pursuits, they (like the dwarves) turn to stone.[7]

Dwarves (*dvergr* may possibly be etymologically related to *draugr*) are older than human beings but younger than the gods and giants. In addition, they are considered more cultivated and are friendlier to humans than are giants. Their special connection to metal makes them skilled smiths (for forging magic swords, making jewelry for the gods, and the like).

Wights seem to be tied to a particular piece of land, for every area has its own "land wights" (*landvættir*). They sometimes behave aggressively toward human beings (as *mein-vættir*, "hostile or mean wights"), killing humans in horrible ways where they can, especially in isolated places.[8]

Water is known to be the element of the nixes, and nixies, as the origin of their name indicates (*nykr*, "water spirit," from the Proto-Indo-European root *neig*ʷ- ,"bathe or wash").

The elves (*álfr*) and *dísir* (singular *dís,* "female being of high rank, goddess, woman") are probably originally the male and female deceased of the Sib. (If this is in fact correct, they should more aptly appear in the previous section, relating to human beings.)

Among the extrahuman entities of lower mythology and religion we should include the bodies of water, mountains, plants (trees), and animals—conjecturally, at any rate, assuming they enjoyed (cultic) worship.[9] Certain wells fall into this category. We can see in the nixies the personified representatives of such wells. Certain animals and trees should be classified here, too, in cases where they were not manifestations or attributes of certain deities and were not consecrated to certain deities (such as the boar as an animal of the fertility god Frey, or the Donar oak that was felled in Geismar by Bonifatius and which was connected to thunder and fertility). Ultimately it is often impossible to determine whether an animal or tree was worshipped for its transcendental qualities (such as potent fertility or life force) or due to its connection to a deity.

The Deities

Here we will present only the most important deities[10] together with the myths in which they play a role. The Old Icelandic sources preserve this mythology for us in a relatively detailed and coherent way. The form in which it is preserved is not ancient and is the result of the systematizing impulses of the late heathen period (in the tenth century) or the industrious, learned compiling of Icelandic Christian antiquarians (in the twelfth and thirteenth centuries). Further, we cannot escape the impression that here and there something may have been parodied with delicious irony or spontaneously added to the material either out of sheer joy in storytelling or a need to systematize. We begin with the northern Germanic tradition of the two divine classes and their battle and reconciliation. We then deal with the individual northern Germanic gods and goddesses and the mythology that relates to them and their individual counterparts (when known) in the southern Germanic realm. Finally, we will look at some deities that are particular to the Continent and to the British Isles.

The Two Divine Classes

As has been noted, the gods are not the oldest of beings. They came into existence after the giants, and they created the world as we know it from the body of a giant whom they had killed. The gods fell prey to the temptations of giantesses. They also instigated the first war in the world. The divine class of the Ases (Old Icelandic *æsir,* singular form *áss*) learned harmful magic (*gandr, seiðr*) from a female member of the other divine class, the Wanes (Old Icelandic *vanir,* singular form *vanr;* the word is probably cognate to modern German *Wonne,* "joy"*), who had prophetic abilities. In turn, they killed her afterward (by stabbing her with spears and burning her). In the resulting antagonisms that erupt between the Wanes and the Ases, the Ases are aggressively pursued and decide to set their residence up as an unassailable fortress. Toward this end, a giant offers to build a fortification for them within a year—provided he is allowed to have his strong stallion help him with the work. Loki (the trickster among the Ases) advises the Ases to accept this additional condition and to promise the giant that if he completes the construction work on schedule, he will receive as compensation the sun, the moon, and the goddess Freyja—a female Wane whom Odin has already had dalliances with across the battle lines. When it becomes apparent that the giant will actually manage to build the fortress in the agreed upon time frame with the help of his stallion, Loki has to transform himself into an alluring mare in order to distract the giant's horse from its work. The giant's stallion runs off after the mare and spends the night chasing her. Now the work begins to fall behind schedule, and the giant sees that he may be cheated out of his reward. He rightfully protests in anger. Reneging on

---

*[The word is likewise cognate to the first element in modern English *winsome.* —*Trans.*]

their oaths, the Ases call for the help of Thor, who promptly slays the giant with his hammer. This is the first instance of divine oath breaking. In the wake of these events, as a pledge to the giants, Odin has to surrender his eye, and Heimdall (the guardian of the Ases) surrenders his hearing (or an ear?), thus signifying a weakening of the gods and their vigilance. This is also the beginning of war (and oath breaking) among humans. The Ases and Wanes are reconciled through a spittle treaty and by exchanging hostages. Yet now that disaster has been released in the world, it will again break out among the gods, take its fateful and fated course, and signal the end of the world and of all beings—the gods included (*ragna rǫk,* the "fate of the gods").[11]

At this point, it has become clear that the gods are powerful (they are stronger and cleverer than the giants), but *in no way are they morally perfect.* They are subject to temptation. Evil (seduction, harmful magic, oath breaking, war) came into the world due to their moral weakness. Because the gods do not constitute clear-cut embodiments of moral principles, they can also only very conditionally be representatives, protectors, or guarantors of moral order. The moral order is primarily guaranteed by the mechanisms and systems of social ties, although the deities existing above these systems may sometimes be connected to this order. Vár (and Thor) are connected to bonds of marriage and thus to the Sib; Tyr is connected to the swearing of oaths and thus to Sib-transcending social ties. Odin is connected to initiation and thus to the *Männerbund.* Broadly speaking, the other deities who receive worship are connected to the cultic community and thus to public order. This illustrates a fundamental difference between Germanic religion and Christianity, for in Christianity, the Christian god is the most perfected conception (as in the writings of Anselm of Canterbury) and, at the same time, the most moral entity imaginable. (See Mark 10:18, which states that no one except God alone can be called good.)

The mythology of a battle and reconciliation between the two groups of gods is evident only among the northern Germanic peoples; there is no corresponding description of the Wanes to be found among the southern and eastern Germanic peoples. On the other hand, there does exist a southern and eastern Germanic correspondence to the Ases, at least in terms of a general designation for a god.* The category of the Wanes consists of the deities who are active in the sphere of eros and fertility (and who are allied with one another through marriages between siblings). The category of the Ases consists of the deities who demonstrate their power through war and governance. Each of these two divine classes probably has a distinct sociocultural background: in the case of the Ases, this is the religion of the warriors and rulers from the first and second estates; for the Wanes, it is the religion of the farmers of the third estate.

Óðinn/Wuotan (from *Wōðanaz, "master of Wōð"); weekday: Wednes-day, Westfalian Gudnes-dag[†12]

As the highest god in the Germanic pantheon, Odin is a war god, which corresponds completely to the eminent ranking accorded to war and battle on the scale of Germanic values. He teaches his protégés a new wedge-shaped battle formation, the so-called swine array (Old Icelandic *svínfylking*), thus insuring victory for them.[13] As a war god, Odin consequently behaves in an amoral (or better, "transmoral") fashion. He goads friends and relatives against one another, thus leading to war and feud. The greatest conflict in the north, the Battle of Brávellir, is Odin's handiwork and his masterstroke. In human form, he kindles hostilities for so long between two kings, Harald Wartooth and his nephew Sigurd

---

*The Old Icelandic word *áss*, "god, member of the *æsir*," derives from an earlier form *ans-. We can see a vestige of this root, *ans-, in German first names that are still common today, such as Ans-helm (Anselm) or Ans-gēr/Ans-gar (Ansgar), which mean "the one whose protector is god" and "spear of god," respectively. [This same root, having lost the -n- as did the Old Icelandic form, is likewise present in older English names like Oswald (meaning "god ruler") and Oscar (meaning "spear of god"). —*Trans.*]

†The basic format followed here in the headings is: (name of god in) Old Icelandic/Old High German (proto-Germanic etymology of name); weekday name(s). The latter are hyphenated to show their compound parts. [In the case of the above entry, *Gudnes-dag* is a southern Germanic dialectal form that is parallel to and cognate with *Wuodanes-dag*. —*Trans.*]

Ring, who are friends as well as relations, that they come to hate one another and are eventually embroiled in a fateful battle.[14] Odin impels men to break their oaths of loyalty. For example, Odin loans a certain Dag his spear and, in defiance of a sworn oath of loyalty, incites him to impale his brother-in-law Helgi "in the fetter grove"—and, no less, at a sacred site. In a breach of retinue loyalty, Odin assumes the form of Harald Wartooth's charioteer and pushes Harald, his retinue lord, out of the battle wagon, slaying him with his own club.[15]

As a war god, Odin is the god of those who die in battle (who are now in Valhalla) and of the *Männerbünde,* whose members represent the dead among the living. These battle dead and their living representatives together make up the wild host (the *wōð,* the "fury") under Odin's command (his name *Wōðanaz means "master of *wōð*"). As the leader of the *Wuothisheer* (the *wuoth* army, the "fury army"), which roars across the open fields at night during winter storms, Odin/Wuotan promotes the fertility of the soil. This corresponds to the folk belief that the raging of the "Wild Army" is a portent for a bountiful year.[16]

As the cult god and first initiate of the *Männerbünde,* and thus their deity of initiation, Odin initially himself underwent the trial of the initiation rite (spear marking, mock hanging). For this reason, he is also known as "Hanging God" (Old Icelandic *hangaguð, hangatýr*). Odin's function as a god of ecstasy, ecstatic poetry, all sorts of shamanistic sorcery, and even black magic, derives from the techniques of visionary and ecstatic consciousness expansion (soul travel) gained through the *Männerbund* initiation ritual and cult rites.[17]

Odin's dealings with the female sex correspond to his "windy" or variable character, as we have come to know him. He seduces a giant's daughter, Gunnlod, robs her of the mead of poetry, the magic drink, the enjoyment of which makes an individual into a poet (Odin is the god of poets), and, to boot, swears a false oath among the giants.[18] On another occasion he rapes a girl named Rinda (an earth goddess). When the girl initially spurns his advances he causes her to go mad through an act of rune magic. Afterward he comes to her in disguise as a healer woman who states that she can heal the girl only after binding her; otherwise the girl will not be able to ingest the necessary bitter medicinal drink. Having accomplished this, Odin rapes and impregnates the bound and defenseless girl.[19]

Odin is described as being one-eyed—as a restless wanderer in a blue cloak, his one-eyed face hidden from view by a wide-brimmed, low-hanging hat.[20] He rides an eight-legged horse (the offspring of a union between Loki as a stallion and the drafthorse of a giant). His animal companions are eagles, ravens, and wolves—in other words, the animals of the battlefield. Ravens are also traveling souls ("soul birds"), which Odin can send out to obtain news from faraway places. The wolves are also animal embodiments of the lawlessness that he continually incites.

Odin's nature is one of wandering, unrest, and the destructive and creative transgression of boundaries. Through war, legal breaches, the censorious actions of the *Männerbund*, ecstasy, magic, and the poetic arts, he repeatedly breaks down the rigid structure of normality. In doing so, he simultaneously makes room for the new, the unheard of, and the uncommon, and for movement and change.

*Týr/Zíu (from *Tīwaz, Teiva, related to Old Indic* devaḥ, *"shining god"); weekday: Tues-day, Allemanic* Zīsch-tig

The Romans saw this god as one that was parallel to their Mars.* At Hadrian's Wall in the third century, Frisian legionary soldiers dedicated an altar with the inscription *Deo Marti Thingso* ("To Mars, God of the Thing").[21] Tīwaz must then have originally been a god of war and of the people's assembly, the Thing, and therefore, he bore the corresponding epithet (*Þingsaz* "god of the Thing"). A vestige of this epithet is evident in the German word for Tuesday,† *Diens-tag*, which originally meant "day of the Thing." As a war god, Tyr was superceded by Odin. This

---

*See the corresponding names for this weekday in various Romance languages: *martedì, mardi,* and so forth.

†[Our English word *Tuesday* evolved from Old English *Tiwesdæg*, "Tiw's day." Tiw is the Old English divine name corresponding to Tyr. —*Trans.*]

came about when *Männerbund*-structured communities were on the verge of making world history with the Viking raids. In runic magic, however, the ↑-rune (Týr rune) continued to be a sign that conferred victory.

As the god of the Thing assembly in the north, Tyr became a god of legal justice and, in particular, a god of oaths. As such, he may have been especially connected to the ring, a legal symbol ("Ring Tyr"*). Tyr is described as the only divine figure who is moral (in *our* sense of morality), because an oath indeed provides one of the few possibilities for cementing stable social ties between members of different Sibs. Further, because Tyr stood by a promise he had given, he forfeited his right hand (the hand for swearing an oath). The thirteenth-century mythographer Snorri Sturluson relates the tale: The gods raise a wolf (the offspring of Loki and a giantess) in their midst, but come to foresee that it will bring them misfortune. As the wolf quickly increases in size and strength, the gods decide to put fetters on him, but how are they to accomplish this? They suggest to the wolf that he should let them put fetters on him as part of a game, so that he could break loose and thus demonstrate his strength to all. The wolf is wary and refuses to agree. The gods suggest that whatever the outcome, the game will be risk-free to the wolf himself. If he is unable to rip apart the fetters, they will set him loose, for this means he is so weak that none should have reason to fear him. If, however, he is able to break loose from the fetters, then this would be a brilliant demonstration of his strength. The wolf agrees to this alleged test of strength on the condition that one of the gods places his right hand in his jaws as a guarantee (a sign that the gods are sincere and that there is no subterfuge involved). Tyr does so, but when the fettered wolf is unable to break free from the magical bands that have been

---

*[The epithet *bauga-tyr*, literally translated as "Tyr of rings" or "god of rings," turns up in stanza 6 of the skaldic poem *Hákonarmál* as an apparent kenning for Generous (or Noble) Man, although it could also be interpreted as "God of (round) Shields" and thus a kenning for *warrior*. It is unclear whether the term has a genuine religious or mythological origin in reference to the god Tyr. —*Trans.*]

fashioned by the dwarves, he snaps shut his jaws—and off comes Tyr's hand. "Then they all laughed except for Tyr."[22]

Þórr/Thonar, Donar (from *Þunaraz, "thunderer"); weekday: Thurs-day, German Donners-tag *(thunder[er]'s day)*

Thor, a very popular deity, is the great strongman among the gods. He is a violent tempered blusterer, a mighty beer drinker, an enormous eater, and a tough warhorse. He primarily fights against the giants: the forces of the sterile, rocky wastelands, winters, and ice storms which constrict and imperil the places inhabited by humans and gods in the north. His weapon is the hammer Mjǫllnir (compare Russian *mólnija,* "lightning"). Thor fights mainly by means of his monstrous strength. By contrast, Odin and Loki make use of war tricks and deception.

Thor is described as youthful, tall in stature, handsome in appearance, and red-bearded.[23] He has a team of goats, which he can ride so swiftly that the mountains crack and fire erupts from the earth. When he is hungry, he can slaughter his goats, cook their meat in a kettle, and devour it. After doing so, if he simply lays out all the bones, undamaged, on the goats' torn-off hides and touches them with his hammer, the animals are brought back to life. One time a young man whom Thor has invited to join him for such a meal splits a thighbone with his knife so that he can suck out the marrow. When Thor touches the hides and bones of the goats with his hammer, as he always does after the meal, one of the resurrected goats turns out to be lame. Thor's anger at this is great, but he lets it be appeased.[24] Underlying this story is an old sacrificial custom according to which the bones of the butchered sacrificial beast should not be broken so that it may be resurrected in the afterlife.[*25] Behind this sacrificial practice is a belief—held by some Indo-European peoples in the Siberian realm and elsewhere—about the possibility of a supernatural (divine) reanimation of the slain bodies

---

*Compare the sacrificial commandment that no bone of the Passover lamb shall be broken (Exodus 12:46).

of humans and animals provided that their bones are kept whole and intact.*[26]

Freyr, Frø (from Fraujaz, "the one who is 'first,' the lord"; compare German Fron, "service to a feudal lord, slavery"; Fron-leichnam, "body of the Lord, Corpus Christi")†

Frey belongs to the divine class of the Wanes; as such he is a fertility god and has a relationship with his sister. Frø is especially worshipped in Sweden, and he has a great temple at Uppsala, where he is allegedly depicted with a giant phallus. There must be obscene aspects to his cult, as is fitting for a fertility god. He bestows peace and pleasure to human beings. Under the name Fróði ("the abundant one, the fertile one") he is connected to a mythical, primordial, and idealized king of peace. The canon Adam of Bremen (d. after 1081), writing in Latin, calls him Fricco, which may indicate that there existed a Germanic familiar form of his name as *friðkā(n), "lover, wooer." If so, this likewise corresponds to his nature as a fertility deity.[27] Apparently, human sacrifices are also offered up to him; he is even said (by Saxo) to have introduced this form of sacrifice.[28] The pig, an animal embodiment of fertility, as well as the horse, are "his" animals. Under threat of malicious magic, Frey makes the giantess Gerd succumb to his will; she is regarded as his wife, for marriage among siblings is seen as disreputable by the Ases.[29]

A Christian tale from the thirteenth century[30] tells of a certain Gunnar Helming who, falling under suspicion of murder in the reign of King Olaf Tryggvason (d. 1000), flees to Sweden, and seeks refuge in a temple dedicated to Frey (Frø). During a cultic procession in wintertime in which an image of Frey is transported around the region in a ceremonial wagon by the temple priestess (who acts as Frey's wife), Gunnar smashes the image of the god, dons the vestments that had

---

*See the well-known fairy tale "The Almond Tree" (Von dem Machandelbaum).
†The format here is Old Icelandic, Old Swedish (proto-Germanic etymology).

adorned it, and assumes its place. When the priestess becomes impreg-
nated by Gunnar, after a time, the people all view this as a portent
of a good year. When Gunnar gets word that the murder allegation
against him is no longer in effect and will not be pursued, he heads off
to Norway with the priestess. As a Christian, in Norway, Gunnar—
together with his wife, the former priestess of Frey—receives baptism.
The tale allows us to discern a heathen custom of cultic processions
with an image of Frey. This was done for the promotion of fertility
and probably also in tandem with the ritual of a cultic marriage—an
act of fertility magic in which the priestess represented and embodied
the wife of the god.

In an Icelandic story from the thirteenth/fourteenth century,[31] a
supposed heathen custom from Norway is depicted in which a horse
phallus wrapped in linen and leeks is passed from hand to hand by a
peasant family every evening in winter. As each person receives the
object, they must utter an obscene poem. It is impossible to tell if this
is a polemical Christian spoof of heathen life or if the verses offer a
glimpse into a family-based Frey cult (Frey's attribute was indeed a
giant phallus, and his cult was described as obscene) from an earlier
period.

Njǫrðr (from *Nerþuz, the original meaning of which is uncertain)

Njǫrðr is a Wane, a fertility deity incestuously involved with his sister
(whose name is not attested in the north). He confers abundance, safe
journeys at sea, and plentiful bounties of fish, and he governs the wind.
His residence is called Nóa-tún (ship town).

Because marriage among siblings is despised by the Ases, Njǫrðr
marries a giant's daughter named Skaði (etymologically related to
"shadow" or "scathe"?). The union is an unhappy one, for the couple
can never agree upon a residence in which they will dwell together, so
they live apart: Skaði in the mountains, where she hunts and skis, and
Njǫrð by the ocean.[32]

Loki (from *Lukā[n], connected to Old Icelandic* lúka, *"to close,"*
in the sense of shutting and bringing to an end)
Loki is an Ase and the son of a giant. He is called the trickster among
the gods. He repeatedly counsels his fellow gods toward undertakings
that threaten to turn out catastrophically for them. He then has to utilize his own cunning to help them out of difficult situations.[33]

Together with a giantess, Angr-Boða ("grief messenger"), Loki
sired three monsters: the Fenris wolf (probably etymologically related
to "fen, marshland"), the Midgard serpent, and Hel. The gods foresaw
that these three monsters would bring them much misfortune. As a
result, they cast the Midgard serpent into the sea (where Thor would
one day clobber it over the head[34]); it lay there, lurking and biting
its own tail. Hel was banished by the gods to Niflheim ("fog home,"
in the icy north); she became both the realm of the dead and goddess of the dead. The Fenris wolf was fettered by the gods with tricks
and treachery, for which Tyr forfeited his right hand.[35] At the end
of the world all three monsters join with their father, Loki (consider
the etymology of his name), to usher in the downfall of the gods and
humans.

Loki's most dire escapade is depicted for us in great detail by
the Icelandic "mythographer" Snorri Sturluson in his work known
as the *Prose Edda*.[36] The myth of Loki's fateful deed revolves around
one of the most significant (and enigmatic) Germanic divine figures:
Baldr, who is probably first literarily attested as Balder in the Second
Merseburg Charm from Germany.*[37] The interpretation of his name is
a subject of debate. It may be related to Lithuanian *báltas* and Russian
bél[yj], "white"—or perhaps to Old Icelandic *baldr,* "brave, bold." The
interpretation of his name may in turn be related to differing argued
interpretations of the myth. Balder, the son of Odin, suffers from bad
dreams portending his death. As a result, his mother, Frigg, has all crea-

---

*The manuscript, which dates from the tenth century (the charm itself is older), is in
the Domstiftsbibliothek at Merseburg. A facsimile of the manuscript is kept on display
there.

tures and things swear an oath that they will not harm Balder. Loki figures out that Frigg has overlooked *one* plant in administering these oaths: the mistletoe (which sprouts shoots only in late fall and has thus been called the "messenger of winter"[38]). The remaining gods, believing Balder to be invulnerable by virtue of the oaths, concoct a game at their gatherings in which they line him up and let him be shot at, hit, and pelted with stones. Loki then counsels Balder's blind brother Hǫðr (related to *hǫð*, "battle") to shoot at him with a twig of mistletoe. This pierces Balder, who falls down dead. Hǫðr must atone for the deed with his own death. Balder is given a sumptuous ship burial (similar to that described by Ibn Faḍlān) in which his wife follows him in to death (*Totenfolge*). Hel, the ruler of the realm of the dead, is entreated by the gods to return Balder to the living. She agrees on the condition that all things, alive and dead, will mourn him. Only one giantess, Þǫkk (her name means "thanks, joy"), refuses to weep. In fact, she is Loki, who has taken on her appearance as a disguise. Because of this, Balder remains in the underworld. The gods capture Loki, who tries to flee after transforming himself into a slippery salmon, and they bind him to a cliff. A snake hanging over him occasionally spits down venom so that he writhes in pain, causing the earth to quake. Loki remains bound in this manner until Ragnarök, at which time he will break free and the current world will come to an end.

Strictly speaking, this mythological story deals with an entire constellation of different, intertwined myths. I will single out two of them here: the myth of Balder's death and that of Loki's binding. In the story of Balder's death, Loki is probably introduced only in a secondary fashion, as the mythic material in Saxo Grammaticus's history may indicate.*[39] We can interpret the history in two ways: in a nature-mythic sense—that is, as a seasonal myth in which the blind Hǫðr, representing the dark season, conquers the god of light, Balder,

---

*His *Gesta Danorum* offers a euhemeristic version of the myth in which Loki does not appear.

who represents the light half of the year—or in a cultic-mythic sense, as an initiation myth, with the test of courage by Balder (the "bold one") and his death at the hands of Hǫðr (the blind "battler") being a reflection of a *Männerbund* initiation ritual and the "little death" that this entails. The scene of the harmless mistletoe transformed into a deadly weapon also fatefully recalls the story in which Víkarr is supposed to be mock hanged in order to secure a favorable journey and dies at the hands of his blood brother Starkad ("strong *hǫðr*"; compare the etymology of Hǫðr) when the reed that Starkad uses to symbolically "spear mark" his mock victim is transformed into a real spear. A myth does not have to be considered so ambiguous that it is impossible for us to favor one of the interpretations (and, admittedly, I lean toward the second one).

The story of Loki's punishment deals with the northern Germanic form of a relatively widespread Indo-European myth. Similar to the bound Loki, who in the end frees himself and joins the side of the enemies of the gods, is the Iranian monster Azdahāg (ḍahḥāk), who (as a result of his horrible misdeeds) is chained to the Damawand (the highest peak of the Alborz mountains), awaiting the moment when he can throw off his fetters and join the fray in the universal final conflict between the evil primordial principle (Ahriman) and the good (Ahura Mazda).[40] Already, here and there, we have come across conspicuous points of contact between the Germanic and Iranian cultural spheres, and we will encounter more of them. Another of Loki's punishments is presented to us more clearly by Saxo and more cryptically by Snorri (and in Icelandic folktales): his outlawry and exile from the inhabited world (Midgard) to the outer world (Utgard), whence his name Útgarða-Loki.[41]

Like Odin, Loki represents the principle of unrest, movement, wandering, and transgression of boundaries. As a consequence some commentators want to view him as simply an aspect—or a kind of split-off personality—of Odin. Yet while Odin's transgressing of boundaries always also unleashes creative impulses, Loki's transgressions tend to lead to catastrophe and destruction. He transforms himself from a god to an "antigod"[42] who sets himself outside the divine order. In this way, though, he becomes the engine of "universal history," an engine that drives to a definitive end (and with it, a totally new beginning) for all things (a "collective eschatology").

Frigg/Frīja (related to Old Indic priyā, "beloved one" and German freien, "to court," and Freier, "suitor, wooer";* weekday: Fri-day, German Frei-tag, Allemanic Frī-tig)

Frigg is the official wife of Odin, a fact that does not deter her from also flirting with other men when opportunities present themselves. A story tells how human beings once gifted Odin with a golden statue of himself. Frigg orders it to be torn down and has jewelry made for herself from the gold; whoever produces this will enjoy her erotic favors. Incidentally, Frigg's rival for Odin, the beautiful Freyja, is spoken of similarly. Odin's wife is also said to have slept with his brothers, her in-laws.[43]

The Old High German translation of the weekday name *dies Veneris* with the term *frīatac* (day of Frīja) proves that Frīja was a love goddess and women's goddess in the southern Germanic realm.

Freyja (from *Fraujōn, "lady," "woman"; female counterpart to Freyr, which derives from *Fraujaz)

Freyja is a Wane and is therefore connected to the sphere of fertility. Along with her twin brother, Frey, she was born of incest between Njǫrðr and his sister. Similarly she was originally in an incestuous relationship with her brother. Alongside this she has a close relationship to Odin, and there is none among the gods who has not been her lover.[†44] Freyja shares the art of malicious magic (*seiðr*) with Odin and in fact is

---

*[The modern German word *Freier* is also used to refer to a "john," or male customer of a prostitute. —*Trans.*]

†Compare the verse mocking Freyja, which was uttered at the Icelandic Althing in the year 999, deriding the goddess as a lewd bitch (*gray*).

said to have taught this form of magic to the Ases.[45] Freyja has animal counterparts that are revealing of her nature as a love goddess and fertility goddess: pigs, cats, and goats.

Like Frigg, Freyja also yearns for adornment. A later (fourteenth-century) mythological farce relates that four dwarves fashion a precious necklace in their smithy. They offer it to Freyja if she will spend a night with each of them. She does so. Odin, angered at this, orders Loki to steal the necklace away from her. Transformed into the shape of a fly, Loki gets into her locked chambers, where she is sleeping with the necklace around her neck. The sleeping goddess, however, is lying on her back, and Loki cannot get at the clasp, which is beneath her neck. Then Loki transforms himself into a flea, bites her on the cheek, and she rolls over and continues sleeping. Now Loki is able to steal the necklace and he departs with it through the chamber door.[46]

It is uncertain whether Gefjon ("giver"), a goddess of fertility and protection, is identical to Freyja or is simply one aspect of her. Also unexplained is the relationship between the northern Germanic goddesses Frigg and Freyja on the one hand, and, on the other, the southern Germanic Frīja (whose name etymologically corresponds to Frigg). Did the southern Germanic Frīja somehow become "doubled" into two goddesses in the north, with one of them (Freyja) then being "fashioned" into a twin sister of the Nordic god Frey (and with both Freyja and Frey apparently lacking any corresponding figures in the southern Germanic realm)? What might call this theory into question is the appearance of pairs of similarly named fertility deities of opposite gender in the southern and northern Germanic spheres (which we will discuss shortly). Or is it the other way around? In this case, the figure of the southern Germanic Frīja represents a coalescence of two goddesses who remained distinct among the northern Germanic peoples, with one of them apparently also corresponding to her linguistically—and all the more so because their functions seems to coincide as well.

Iðunn (etymologically uncertain; probably meaning "the renewing one"[47])

Idun possesses the golden apples, which the gods eat whenever they begin to age; by doing this they remain young until Ragnarök. The apple is a symbol of life and fertility. (In some fairy tales and legends eating an apple causes pregnancy.[48]) Apples are used to decorate Christmas trees as a symbol of life in renewal.

Reverting to much older mythological material, probably even dating from antiquity (the apples of the Hesperides), Snorri Sturluson provides a tale of the abduction of Idun and her apples by Loki, who has been forced to do this by a giant. As a result, the gods quickly start to become gray and old. They then force the cunning Loki to recapture Idun and her apples, and the gods kill the giant.[49]

Nerthus (*Nerþuz, corresponding to Old Icelandic Njǫrðr; probably related to a Proto-Indo-European root *ner-, "under, below," the same root as in the word north, for the underworld was believed to be located in the north[50])

Tacitus refers to a Germanic goddess who is worshipped collectively (that is, through a cultic society) by a federation of Ingvaeonic tribes. He gives her name—Nerthus—and interprets it as meaning "Mother Earth" (terra mater). Her temple is located on an island in the sea. At certain times (probably coinciding with the appearance of new vegetation in the spring), the priests transport her in a wagon to the tribes as part of a ceremonial procession. During this time, peace reigns. Before the goddess is returned to her temple, her image and implements are washed by slaves in a lake. Afterward, the slaves are drowned because they have gazed upon the goddess.[51]

Nerthus (*Nerþuz) was nothing other than the earlier Germanic feminine form of Old West Norse* Njǫrðr. Because the categories of words known as feminine and masculine u-stems are indistinguishable

---

*[Old West Norse is the North Germanic dialect comprising Old Icelandic and Old Norwegian. —Trans.]

in their inflection,* a later North Germanic linguistic development of the feminine form would have likewise had to have been Njǫrðr—and therefore if the god Njǫrðr might have had a sister and feminine counterpart (as Frey has in Freyja), she would have had the same name as him. Because both deities (Nerthus and Njǫrðr) have a connection to fertility (compare, too, the likely etymology of the name, which relates to a notion of "below") and are associated with the sea, the situation could be that in Nerthus we have an attestation for the early form of the name for Njǫrðr's twin sister, whose existence is indeed preserved in the North, although her name, which would also be reconstructed as Njǫrðr, is not recorded. Or it could be the other way around: in Njǫrðr we have a late form of the name for the twin brother of Nerthus, who would have also been called *Nerþuz, but of whose existence Tacitus did not preserve any record.

Besides Frey and Freyja and Njǫrðr and Njǫrðr (*Nerþuz, masculine, and *Nerþuz, feminine), there is a further pair of identically named gods of opposite gender which appears in the Second Merseburg Charm: Phol and Volla (transcriptions for Old High German Fol and Folla, both meaning "full"), whose name indicates a fertility function, and the female version of which appears in the northern Germanic realm as Fulla. This may be an indication that we are on the right track concerning Nerthus/Njǫrðr.

A manifestation of "Mother Earth" (eorðan† modor) is also found in the form of Erce in the so-called Anglo-Saxon Field Blessing (recorded

---

*[Historical linguists traditionally group Germanic words into different categories according to their earliest reconstructed forms; in the case of nouns and adjectives, these categories were determind by the presence of a particular vowel in the word's stem. One of these categories is the u-stem noun, of which there were masculine, feminine, and neuter varieties. In proto-Germanic, the masculine and feminine u-stem nouns were inflected identically for grammatical case, such as here in the nominative, which is marked by a *-z ending. Over many centuries of linguistic development, this ending changed in sound to become a final -r in Old Norse, as we see in Njǫrðr. —Trans.]

†Here with eorðan in the defining genitive (and not meaning "mother of the earth"!); compare Randolph Quirk and C. L. Wrenn, An Old English Grammar, 2nd edition. (London: Methuen, 1960), 62.

around the year 1000, but older[52]): the goddess is invoked to become fertile through God's embrace—and she is invoked by the insular descendants of the same tribes, namely the Angles (Anglii) and the Jutes (Eudoses) that had formerly worshipped Nerthus as "Mother Earth" (*terra mater*) on the Continent. It would be satisfying, then, if we could find certain characteristics of a heavenly god in the postulated companion of Nerthus, the male Nerthus, but such features are lacking both in the etymology of his name (which is nevertheless uncertain) as well as in the North Germanic figure of Njǫrðr himself (apart from his rule over the winds of the sea).

The Alcis (related to "elk"—or to a proto-Indo-European root *alek-, "to defend against, to protect"; compare Old Saxon and Old High German alah, "protected site, temple")

According to Tacitus, certain Germanic peoples worshipped a pair of same-sex twins and male youths.[53] They were called the Alcis (or Alces?), and although they were indigenous deities, from a Roman point of view (*interpretatio romana*) they were similar to the divine twins Castor and Pollux.

Divine pairs of male same-sex twins, which were active as helpers in need, were also known and popular among other Indo-European peoples (the Dioscuri among the Greeks, the Aśvinau among the Indians). The connections between such divine twins and fast draft or riding animals (in the case of the Dioscuri), or to an actual animal form (Aśvinau is related to Sanskrit *aśvaḥ,* "horse"), as well as a connection to a protective function, make both interpretations for the name Alcis ("elk" and "protection") seem reasonable. Ambiguities such as this illustrate the limitations of etymological attempts at explanation.

The Mothers (Matronae/Matres)

Between the first and fourth to fifth centuries of the common era in the Continental western Germanic territory and in particular among the tribe of the Ubii dwelling on the left side of the Rhine (approximately between Bonn and Xanten), consecration stones were erected to female deities. The patrons who sponsored these monuments were native inhabitants of the area as well as Romans; men and women; common people as well as members of the upper classes, the governing bureaucracy, and the military. The deities were called Matronae or Matres (Matrons or Mothers).[54] For the most part, they are depicted in groups of three, typically as three seated female figures in native (that is, non-Roman) dress. Two of them are usually recognizable as women by their bonnets; they flank a younger maiden with uncovered hair. All of them hold baskets of fruit on their laps, in particular apples, pears, and quinces. Evidently, these deities were seen and worshipped as bestowers of fertility, blessings, and happiness.

The oldest datable consecration stone in the Ubii territory (for it refers to the Roman consul of 164 CE) is dedicated to the Aufaniae.*[55] The inscription reads: MATRONIS / AVFANIABVS / Q. VETTIVS SEVERVS / QVAESTOR C.C.A.A. / VOTVM SOLVIT L.M. / MACRINO ET CELSO COS (*"To the Aufanian Mothers has Quintus Vettius Severus, quaestor in Cologne, fulfilled his vow willingly and in accordance with [their] merit under the consulate of Macrinus and Celsus"*).

The Cologne finance official named here had appealed to the Aufaniae entreatingly with a request. As a result of their response, he praised them by erecting a stone with an inscription. The stone and inscription attest that the Matronae were gracious to him.

The most frequently preserved Matronae name is that of the Aufaniae.[56] The difficulty of interpreting this name throws light on the lack of an adequate religious-historical classification for the Matronae deities in general. An etymological connection has been proposed between the name Aufaniae and the tribe of the Ubii. If this is the case, then the Aufaniae were akin to the "tribal mothers" of the Ubii. A different theory connects the name linguistically to the Gothic word *ufjō* ("superfluity, abundance, excess"); the Aufaniae would then be the "Augmentresses" (in other words, "those who bring increase"). Recently

---

*The stone is now in the Rheinisches Landesmuseum in Bonn.

the name has been associated with "fen" (swamp). *Au-fanja* would then refer to the "remote fen," but what does a remote and impassable swamp or an infertile, barren moor have to do with the baskets full of fruit? The overflowing fruit baskets make the Aufaniae seem better interpreted as the Plentiful Ones, the Augmentresses, those who bring increase.

Ēastre, Ēostra (related to a Proto-Indo-European root *aus-, "to shine")

This goddess of the (dawning) light, of increasing daylight and thus of spring and (self-renewing) fertility, is attested among the Anglo-Saxons. The name Easter, which was applied to the Christian festival, was probably borrowed from her.

Lollus, Löllus, Lullus (related to German lallen, "babble"; South Allemanic Lōli, "one who is not in control of his or her tongue, a yokel," and Läli, with the same sense, but also with the meaning "tongue"*)

In his *Sagenschatz des Frankenlandes,* a compendium of local legends from Franconia, Bechstein records:

> One may still read of an alleged heathen idol, whose kind and name belong uniquely to land of the Franks. This is Lollus, Löllus, or Lullus, whose specific worship is said to have occurred along the Main River (near the location of the later city of Schweinfurt). A bronze image of the idol has been found, depicted as a youth with golden hair and curls. A wreath of poppy heads hung around the neck and down across the chest. With its right hand, the figure grasped at its mouth and held the *tongue* between its thumb and forefinger; in its left hand it holds a wine cup containing stalks of grain. The body was completely naked except for an apron around

---

*[Similar cognates exist in English: northern British English dialectal *lolly,* "tongue"; the old-fashioned expression *loll,* "to thrust out (the tongue) in a pendulous manner"; and the first part of the very familiar word *lollipop.* —Trans.]

the loins. The image is said to have stood in a sacred, enclosed grove adjacent to the bank of the river Main and at certain times bunches of grapes and ears of grain were brought to it as offerings by the people.[57]

Recently Loll has been interpreted as the fertility god who is called Freyr in the north and whose name would have been Frō (Lord) in the linguistic area where Old High German was spoken, although this name is not attested in the southern Germanic area in reference to a god. The name Loll (which apparently describes one who "lolls," who is unable properly to use his tongue yet) refers to a very young, infantile vegetation god who may have been connected to Frīja in a sort of mother-son relationship—similar to that which we find with some Oriental mother goddesses and their young son-lovers. In the southern Germanic realm a mother-child relationship (Frīja–Loll) would then be the counterpart to the brother-sister relationship in the North (Freyja–Frey).[58]

With this "speculative finale," our review of the Germanic deities comes to a close. Yet there is still room for another observation. With regard to the deities, it seems that the sphere of fertility is better and more variably represented in the southern Germanic area than it is in the north. This may result from the fact that the Nordic sources, although also piecemeal, reflect—or at least attempt to reflect—the concerns of the warlike Viking Age. As a consequence, the depiction of the "third estate" (that is, the farmers and peasantry) and its typical expressions of religious life have become reshaped by the ideology of both of the classes (the ruling nobility and the warrior class) that exist above it.

The Power of Fate

The deities are not the highest and the ultimate powers. Together with human beings and supernatural beings the gods are also subject to the fate that drives the present world unavoidably toward its end. In the north, this is called the "fate of the gods" (*ragna rǫk*). Even Odin himself is unable to alter fate. His shamanistic abilities simply put him in a position to know it in greater detail. For example, he can certainly ride down to the underworld and, with a waking charm (*valgaldr*), force a (long-dead) seeress (*vǫlva*) there to rise from her grave in order to find out Balder's fate. He can not, however, alter that fate.[59]

As the highest power, fate was sometimes depicted as an impersonal, abstract entity. Words used to refer to it include Old Icelandic *urðr*, Old High German *wurt* (and also *we-wurt*, "woe[ful]-fate"; see p. 54), Old English *wyrd* (which are all etymologically related with modern German *werden*, "to become, to turn into"), as well as Old Icelandic *mjǫtuðr*, Old Saxon *metod*, and Old English *me(o)tod* (which are all etymologically related to our verb *mete*). These terms therefore have the sense of that which "becomes," that which "is measured out." In the Old English epic *Beowulf*, both expressions are used together, and at one point they are mutually explanatory: *wyrd* is the "*metod* of each man" (*metod manna gehwæs*).[60]

Sometimes fate is personified. In the north, people spoke usually of the female "fates," the Norns (Nornar; the etymology is uncertain), as a group of three: Urð, Verðandi, and Skuld (the names can be interpreted as "Has Become," "Becoming," and "Should Occur": past, present, and future?). They firmly set down fate using the same rune magic divination by lots that is familiar to us from Tacitus.[61] In establishing an individual's "lot," the last of the Norns usually acts the most begrudgingly—a trait that has carried on in fairy tales (such as with the gift of the wicked fairy in *Sleeping Beauty*).[62] The trinity of the Norns is reminiscent of the trinity of the Matrones. Indeed, the picture becomes blurred when Saxo[63] reports about a temple of the gods (*deorum edes*), an oracle site of the Norns (*oracula Parcarum*), inside of which three young women (*nymphae*) were found on three seats, and where an individual could inquire about the future destiny of children after ceremonially completing certain vows. It is possible that six hundred years before Saxo, a temple of the Matrones might have had a similar appearance, but there is nothing known to us regarding any temple-based cult of the Norns that involved vows.

Among the religions of the Indo-European peoples there is a noticeable tendency to view the colorful and intricate workings of the deities as subject to higher ordering powers. In India, for example, the gods are subordinate to *ṛtam* ("right order") and, later, to *karma* (the universal principle of repayment for actions committed). In ancient Iran the gods are subordinate to the principle of time (Zurvan was "time," a god of time) that ordains and preordains all. Among the Greeks, the gods are subject to Moîra ("portion, that which is allotted to each person"; a goddess of fate); and among the Romans, to the unavoidable, all-governing *fātum* ("fate decreed"). It is in this Indo-European context that we should understand the higher-ranked position of the power of fate in relation to all other powers among the Germanic peoples.[64] And this helps us understand the attraction that the Christian god held for the people of antiquity and for the Germanic peoples. The Christian god is the lord of fate, for in his hands rests the "destiny of every human being" (*metod*) and even *wyrd* itself: without his willful cooperation, "no sparrow falls from the sky and no hair falls from the head" (Matthew 10:29–30). What could have better demonstrated his superiority over the old gods than this? Further, how could it have been better expressed in words than in an Old English Christian hymn from around 670 CE (one of the oldest examples of vernacular poetry north of the Alps) that transfers the name of fate (*metod*) to God and praises God's power as *"metudæs mæcti"*?*[65]

Interacting with Fate

A person's religious bearing toward a power (or powers) could manifest in various ways: subjugation, ritual effort (rites of passage, magic), or cultic worship. In practice these forms were hard to differentiate, but generally and broadly speaking, the powers of fate demanded subjugation, the deities were offered cultic worship, and human and superhuman entities were dealt with through rituals.

---

*[The Old English phrase can be literally translated "God's might." —*Trans.*]

When confronted with fate, a human being has no choice but to submit. A person can indeed make use of rituals, namely magic (runic magic, death magic, divinatory magic), to ascertain his or her fate, but fate cannot be altered.[66] Even the gods are unable to do that. Admittedly Saxo may provide evidence for cultic worship of the Norns—presuming his account actually concerns the female fates.

A human being as such was not an object of cultic worship for the Germanic peoples. A person's life and death had to be accompanied by rituals, however, if the individual was to be successful. A person could also influence other people through rituals—by manipulating them magically (such as with harmful magic or love magic). A person could also exert ritual influence upon himself or herself, inducing superhuman power through specific ritual techniques. In certain cases, however, *dead* human beings seem to have enjoyed cultic worship: the Nordic sources mention sacrifices to the elves and the *dísir*, but these references are too scant, too unreliable and lacking in detail, to allow for any clear picture of these cultic activities.[67] We also must make the further assumption that the elves and *dísir* actually represented male or female deceased members of the Sib. The Norwegian king Halfdan the Black, during whose reign fertility was thought to have ascended to an unparalleled degree, was allegedly quartered after his death so that each section of his body could be buried in a different part of southeastern Norway, because each region hoped to have bountiful years ahead if it received a portion of the dead king.[68]

Because the land wights were largely perceived as being hostile toward humans, rituals were required for situations when keeping company with them seemed unavoidable. The tenth-century Úlfljótr, which is probably the oldest law of Iceland, required that the carved dragon images on the prows of ships be removed when the ships called in at harbor so that the land wights would not be disturbed by the open jaws on the dragon heads (and react with corresponding aggression).[69] In order to provoke the land wights into behaving aggressively against someone and driving them from the land, the wights had to be charmed (threatened) with cursing magic.[70] Magic was also employed for dealing with giants.

Magical knowledge enables a young hero to resist a lustful giantess who wants to sleep with him; he does this by stringing her along until daybreak, when the sunlight turns her to stone.[71] By carving death runes (*hel-stafir,* "Hel staves") and directing them at the giantess, the recalcitrant man can make her oblivious to the deadly danger awaiting her.[72] As we have already discussed, it is possible that elves and *dísir* are the objects of cultic worship (sacrifice), but we can say nothing more precise.

The cultic worship of a mountain is attested in Iceland. A Germanic cult surrounding wells or springs is indicated by the archaeological finds of votive offerings that were deposited at such locations.[73] The worship of plants and animals in connection to a deity can be considered an aspect of honoring that particular deity and therefore do not qualify as the worship of organic objects per se. The remaining reports that are left to us which refer in some way to pure animal and plant worship may represent misunderstandings on the part of their Christian authors. Such material is therefore difficult to evaluate.[74]

The deities receive cultic worship (through sacrifice, prayer, or other ceremonial acts performed either in the context of the Sib or through the activities of a cultic society, and usually at specific times and places). Because cultic worship also makes use of rituals (and sorcerous and magical elements) in order to function smoothly and be efficacious, overlapping gray areas result (for example, between death penalties and sacrifices, between magical charms and prayers, and between magical rituals and festive proceedings). We should take into account these gray areas when we interpret such activities.

Wherever it is practiced, the loftiest and most effective offering to a deity is a human sacrifice. By sacrificing a king or a young human being, an especially large amount of vitality is conveyed to the deity. Human sacrifice is well attested among the Germanic peoples, as is royal sacrifice. Odin and Frey distinguished themselves in particular as recipients of human sacrifices. This was probably true of Nerthus as well—presuming that in Nerthus's case it was not simply a situation in which slaves were killed in order to keep a secret. Among the Frisians, boys and youths seem to have had particular prestige as worthy "sac-rificial material."[75] We can see mock hanging in tandem with spear marking (also practiced as an initiation rite) as a diluted or somehow "homeopathically rarefied" form of human sacrifice—although in the account that is left to us (see p. 40), the mock sacrifice turns out to be a tragic flop because it miscarries. On the picture stone of Lärbro Hammars I (erected around the year 700 on the island of Gotland), we can see a visual depiction of a human sacrifice to Odin. The depiction shows an altarlike structure on which a cultic figure (perhaps a priest) marks a prostrate sacrificial victim with a spear. At the left, a warrior in full armor (with sword and shield) is hanging from the downward-bent crown of a tree. At the right, a procession of armed men appears, and the foremost of these presents a powerful bird of prey (probably an eagle, an animal connected to Odin*). The image on the stone seems to depict three acts of sacrificial performance that follow one another: procession, spear marking, and hanging.[76] A sacrifice to Odin was also certainly at the origins of the practice of "carving the blood eagle"(rísta blóðǫrn) which served as a deadly form of torture during the Viking Age:[77] the back of a (still-living) sacrificial victim was sliced open, the ribs were separated from the spine and bent forward, and the lungs were pulled out in such a way that they formed a pair of "wings"on the vic-tim's back. This transformed the victim into a quasi-sacrificial bird, a "blood eagle" that was thus offered up to Odin.[78] The sacrificial for-mula used to offer a human sacrifice to Odin must have been something along the lines of: "Now I give you to Odin!" (Nú gef ek þik Óðni!)[79]

We have already come across various sacrificial animals such as horses, cattle, and sheep (offered together with vegetables and food and drink that did not require bloodshed; see p. 14), goats, and eagles. Another sacrificial animal is the boar.†[80] A deity is most effectively

---

*[One of the Old Icelandic by-names for Odin is arnhǫfði, "the eagle-headed one." —Trans.]

†A "descendant" of the Yule boar described here is the Swedish Christmas pig. Com-pare also the depictions of pigs on the south interior wall of the Ringebu stave church in Gudbrandstal.

strengthened through a sacrifice of the animal that represents their essence and that is seen as a manifestation of it (two related Germanic terms for *sacrifice* are Old Icelandic *blóta* and Old High German *bluozan*, both of which probably derive from a proto-Indo-European root **bhel-/bhlō-*, "to swell, to grow abundantly," and thus have the basic meaning of strengthening the deity). The optimal sacrifice to a god or goddess is therefore his or her particular animal: for Odin, this is the horse (and eagle?); for Frey, the boar (and horse); for Thor, the goat. The cultic celebrants who communally ingested the sacrificial meat partook of a portion of the deity's essence conveyed through the medium of the animal that incorporate that essence.[81] The most detailed portrayal of an Icelandic sacrificial ceremony comes from the temple description that appears in the *Eyrbyggja saga* (The Saga of the People of Eyr), recorded in the thirteenth century.[82] This description, and another description in a later saga (unrelated to the *Eyrbyggja saga*), apparently trace back to Snorri Sturluson's report about a sacrificial feast at Lade (today, a suburb of Trondheim, Norway).[83] Snorri's report, however, is suspected of fancifully incorporating Old Testament sacrificial customs and Christian liturgy in its portrayal of a heathen sacrificial ceremony of the tenth century. This was a ceremony of which Snorri would no longer have had any direct knowledge, or, if he did, he does not make use of such knowledge in his portrayal.[84] In Snorri's account, for example, a *hlaut-teinn*—a "twig" (compare Alemannic dialectal *Zeine,* "a laundry basket woven from twigs"*) used for the casting of lots (rune staves used for divination by lots) has its function abruptly shifted to that of an aspergillum as used in the Christian liturgy. Using this *teinn,* the blood of the sacrificial animal is alleged to have been sprinkled on the altar, the cultic celebrants, and the temple walls following the example of Old Testament rites (Exodus 24:6, 8; Exodus 12:22).[85]

The type of building described in the *Eyrbyggja saga* as a temple has indeed been excavated; it corresponds to a large Icelandic farmhouse (in

---

*[A direct cognate is also found in archaic English *tine,* a "small branch or twig." —*Trans.*]

which cultic activities certainly could have been held). Yet this, therefore, provides us with little information about buildings that might have
been specifically designed for cultic use. The best examples of how heathen sacred buildings in the north might have looked are provided to us
by the Norwegian stave churches (Borgund, Heddal, Hedalen, Urnes,
Lom, among others). Their perfection in terms of craftsmanship and
elaborate ornamentation would then not simply be due to the highly
developed woodworking technology of the Viking Age,*[86] but instead
were the result of a long and wonderful tradition of carpentry used for
sacred buildings.

In the southern Germanic realm, Pope Gregory the Great's direc-
tive from the year 601, which instructs missionaries not to destroy heathen holy sites but instead to convert them into Christian churches if
the existing structures are well built,[87] may illustrate that, in any event,
there were heathen temples destroyed in the course of the Christian
mission, and in cases where they were not destroyed, Christian
churches took their places over time. In the southern Germanic territories, therefore, we know almost nothing more precise about the
way in which temples were built. Wood, which is a perishable building
material (in contrast to the stone used for Christian churches), may
have been a part of the earlier building tradition.[88] A further issue is
the fact that the Germanic peoples—who were similar to the ancient
Iranians in this respect—liked to worship their deities at particular sites (*luci ac nemora*, "in forest clearings") under the open sky.[89]
Tacitus mentions a grove in which the Semnones held public human
sacrifices and which was said to be so sacred that it could be entered
at other times only if an individual was bound in fetters (in order
not to weaken the power of the place). A person who fell down there
was not allowed to stand up; he was allowed only to roll away on the
ground.[90] In the *Lay of Helgi* (written more than one thousand years
after Tacitus's time), a "fetter grove" (*fjǫtur-lundr*) is mentioned.

*[Many commentators believe the most impressive products of this technology are found
in the examples of Viking shipbuilding. —*Trans.*]

This grove thus shares a similar taboo with the one referred to by Tacitus, though of course the two sites should not be seen as identical in form to one another.

In cases where archaeological evidence is lacking for former cult sites, research into place names can provide clues. For example, place names whose first component can be traced to an old divine name (for example, Thor or Odin) and whose second component consists of *lundr* (grove) or *vé* (holy site), such as Tollund (from Thors-lund) or Odense (from Odens-vi) in Denmark, suggest that they once referred to pre-Christian groves or temples. The same principle is naturally valid for the other Germanic linguistic areas.

Processions and supplications were also part of public cult activities. The Anglo-Saxon Field Blessing is a supplication from a public cultic event[91]—and one in which the boundary between a magical charm (*gealdor**) and a prayer is blurred:

> *Earth I pray to and heaven above* (up-heofon) . . .
> *Erce, Erce, Erce, Mother Earth!*
> *May the all-powerful Eternal Lord grant you*
> *fields, growing and thriving,*
> *flourishing and bountiful* . . .
> *and [bright shafts] of white wheat*
> *and all fruits of the earth* . . .
> *Hail to you, earth, mother of men*
> *May you be growing in God's embrace,*
> *filled with food for the benefit of men.*

The practice of private prayer† is described to us by Ibn Faḍlān. In terms of the Sib and the household, we have seen private sacrificial

---

*The word occurs in the preface to the Field Blessing, which is not reproduced here.
†Compare the Roman bronze figure of a "praying German" (Germanic tribesman) in the Bibliotèque Nationale, Paris. See Klaus Bemmann, *Der Glaube der Ahnen: Die Religion der Deutschen, bevor sie Christen wurden* (Essen: Phaidon, 1990), 121–22, figure 30.

activities and cultic proceedings in forms such as the sacrifices to the elves and *dísir* and in the rite involving the horse phallus. In the case of sacrifice to the elves the reports concerning such private practices are not very informative; in the rite involving the horse phallus, the story itself is not particularly believable.

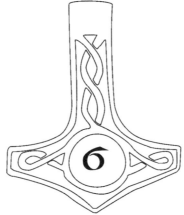

The Conception of the World (Cosmography)

The Old Icelandic sources present us with three different cosmographical models[1] that can be established from the mythological data. These models contain uncertainties, contradictions, and overlapping elements, and it is difficult to come to any definitive conclusions about the age of the respective cosmographies.

The humans and gods inhabit a world (the first component of our word *world* comes from *wer*, "man, human being") called Mið-garðr (the "'middle' region"; with regard to the second component, compare the modern English word *garden**). Outside of Midgard is Ut-garðr, the outer world, which is home to giants and troublesome creatures. Midgard is surrounded by a primordial ocean that forms a ring around it. The monstrous Midgard serpent dwells in this ocean, biting its own tail. It was cast there by the gods.

A second cosmographical model situates Midgard in the west and Utgard (or Jǫtun-heimr, "giants' home") in the east. The two realms are

---

*[Consider, too, another etymologically related word in English: *yard*. In both cases, the sense is of an enclosed area used for human or domestic activities. —*Trans.*]

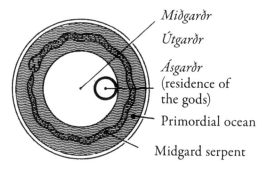

Midgarðr
Útgarðr
Ásgarðr
(residence of
the gods)
Primordial ocean
Midgard serpent

Model 1

separated by a river or river system, Éli-vágar (probably meaning "storm sea"), and a forest, Járn-viðr (iron forest).

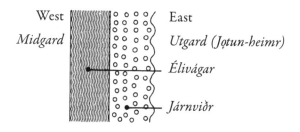

West
Midgard

East
Utgard (Jǫtun-heimr)
Élivágar
Járnviðr

Model 2

The third model depicts the universe as a cosmic tree (World Tree). Its three underground roots comprise the realm of the dead, the realm of the giants, and the realm of human beings. The tree's branches in the heavens contain the realm of the gods. Between the realm of the gods and the realm of human beings spans the rainbow bridge, Bif-rǫst (trembling, swaying path?) or Ás-brú (bridge of the Ases): the gods ride over it to the realm of the humans, the initiates fare across it on shamanistic soul journeys, and the dead heroes[2] use it to reach finally the world of the gods. The cosmic tree is described as an ash and is called Yggdrasill. Its interpretation as Odin's (Ygg's: the "Terrible One's") horse, allegedly a reference to Odin's aerial ride on the tree (and thus to his initiation through mock hanging as the first initiate) seems like a folk etymology, and is unsatisfactory.* A dragon gnaws at the roots of Yggdrasill: the World Tree's stability is continually threatened by this, and its life span is limited.

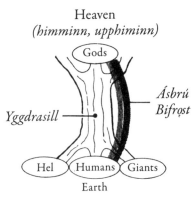

Heaven
(*himminn, upphiminn*)

Gods

Ásbrú
Bifrǫst

Yggdrasill

Hel   Humans   Giants

Earth

Model 3

At best, some fragments of this cosmographical model from the north can be found in the southern Germanic realm. In the Old High German text "Muspilli," we find the words *mittilagart* and *himil* (the latter of which appears in the Old High German "Wessobrunn Prayer" as *ufhimil.*[†]) In the Old English poem "Cædmon's Hymn" we find the corresponding terms *middungeard* and *heben* (*heofon*); the poem says that heaven (*heben*) arches over the earth like a roof (*hrof*), which is why in other places it is also called *upheofon* (upper heaven).[3] The Norse World Tree has its iconic counterpart in the famed Irminsul destroyed by Charlemagne during the capture of Eresburg (now Obermarsberg, North Rhine-Westphalia, Germany). The Benedictine monk Rudolf of Fulda (d. 865) describes the Irminsul as a large tree trunk (*truncus*) erected under the open sky, and he translates its indigenous name, *Irmin-sul* (the first component perhaps coming from proto-Germanic

---

*[A folk etymology is an assumed word etymology that has gained popular currency (often subsequently influencing the sound and appearance of the word itself), but which is ultimately incorrect from a historical-linguistic standpoint. —*Trans.*]

†[Literally, "up(per)-heaven," or, we might say, "heaven on high." —*Trans.*]

erminaz, "high" or "all-encompassing"*), with the phrase "universal column" (*universalis columna*), because it was said in a sense to support everything.[4] This brings us back again to the northern Germanic peoples and to heathen Uppsala in Sweden where, according to Adam of Bremen, there stood a giant, broadly outstretched evergreen tree, the species (*genus*) of which no one knew[5]—a microcosmic manifestation of the universe in the form of a tree. Conceptualizing the universe as a tree is also well documented in the Asiatic (Siberian, Indo-Iranian) sphere, and the myth of the World Tree has its ritual counterpart in shamanistic practices: using the technique of soul travel, a shaman is able to ascend the World Tree and (in the interest of and as a duty to the community) interact with the various nonhuman realms.

---

*[The second component, *sul,* is cognate with modern German *Säule,* "pillar, column." —*Trans.*]

The Beginnings of Time
and the End Times

The individual acts in the dramas of the creation and destruction of the world are preserved for us in the Old Icelandic sources.*[1] These have parallel conceptions in the Indo-Iranian sphere that match them point for point. Moreover, the scenario of the destruction of the world proceeds just as it does in the apocalyptic texts of the New Testament. This is what we will now examine.

Creation

In the beginning, there "existed" a primordial vacuum (*ginnunga-gap*, "yawning void";† compare modern English *gap*). The world was formed from the body of a slain primordial giant whose name (Ymir) means "twin" or "hermaphrodite." The earth was created from his flesh, the

---

*Especially the poem *Vǫluspá* (The Seeress's Prophecy); compare also the discussion of the *vǫlva* on p. 81. [In the English title of the text, the word "seeress" translates Old Icelandic *vǫlva*. —*Trans.*]

†[The name has also been etymologically explained by Jan De Vries as having the sense of the "magically charged void." See the entries for "Ginnungagap" in Simek, *Dictionary of Northern Mythology,* and Vries, *Altnordisches etymologisches Wörterbuch,* 2nd edition (Leiden: Brill, 1977). —*Trans.*]

ocean from his blood, the mountains from his bones, the trees from his hair, and the (vaulted) heavens from his skull.[2] Tacitus mentions that a "first being" named Tuisto ("Hermaphrodite," related to proto-Germanic *twi-, "two"; compare also modern German *Zwitter,* "hermaphrodite"), an origination deity and earth deity, is a subject of ancient Germanic songs.[3] The concepts of a primordial vacuum and the creation of the world from a slain giant (a primordial being) are known in both the Indian and Iranian spheres.

The gods created human beings from two plants, Askr (which means "ash tree") and Embla (which perhaps means "vine"). The creation of human beings from a pair of plants is a set feature of the Iranian mythology concerning primordial times.

Götterdämmerung (Twilight of the Gods)*

Distinct from individual eschatology (the complex of beliefs concerning the fate of the individual after his or her death) is the so-called collective eschatology that deals with the fate of the entire world and all its creatures. Time and again in our examination of Germanic religion, we have encountered notions that allude to a future and predetermined end for everything that exists. Such notions are quite evident in the depiction of the deities, in the early understanding of the power of fate, and with regard to the World Tree. Until now, however, we have observed these ideas only among the northern Germanic peoples. As mentioned at the outset of this chapter, the scenario of world destruction portrayed for us in these sources is not only paralleled scene-for-scene in the Iranian (and Indian) texts but also in the apocalypses of the New Testament.

The drama of the end times proceeds with the dissolution of all forms of human community: brother will fight against brother, the

---

*Ragnarøkkr ("Götterdämmerung" or "twilight of the gods") is a late reinterpretation of the term ragna rǫk (meaning "fate of the gods") and it was then absorbed into modern usage. Compare also Richard Wagner's "Ring Cycle."

bonds of the Sib will be torn apart, and loyalty will be breached—and in these ways the mechanisms and systems of social ties will collapse. Exactly the same scenario occurs in the Iranian end times mythology and in Mark 13:12. (It occurs similarly in the Indian doctrine of the Yugas, or world historical ages.)

The destruction of social ties serves as the prelude to the catastrophe that follows. The fettered countervailing power, Loki, enemy of the gods and humans, breaks loose togther with his demonic brood (the Fenris wolf and the Midgard serpent). The serpent is similar to the Iranian monster Azdahāg and to Satan, who is referred to as the "dragon" and the "old serpent" in the final book of the Bible (Revelation 20:7). (Indian mythology foretells of devastating cyclical outbreaks of demons, who are contrary to the gods, from their banishing place under the earth.)

The situation escalates into an unavoidable and violent confrontation between the gods and their opponents (Loki, his clan, the giants). Odin, Tyr, Thor, and Frey are killed, as are Loki, the Fenris wolf, and the Midgard serpent. An analogous final duel takes place in the Iranian depiction of the end times under the rubric of the Great Battle (*Ardīg ī Wuzurg*). In the Christian apocalypse (Revelation 20:8–10) there is the violent battle (staged by the devil) of Gog and Magog against Jerusalem and its saints. (In India this event is incorporated into the doctrine of the world historical ages.)

Climatic and cosmic catastrophes destroy the old existing creation: a terrifying winter comes;[4] the sun is eclipsed, the heavenly bodies fall to earth, the earth sinks into the sea, fire devastates the universe (incinerating the World Tree[5]). Again, there are parallel conceptions to these events in the Iranian and Christian apocalyptic texts (Mark 13:24–25; Revelation 11:6; and 2 Peter 3:10). (In India the cyclical destruction of the universe is described with the same stock of images.)

Creation is then renewed: a new earth arises out of the sea, the unsown fields bear fruit. The sole survivors are the sons of Odin and Thor; Balder and Hǫðr come back to life. A pair of human beings is formed from the (new) World Tree, and these are the parents of a new humanity.*[6] The Iranian drama of the end times also concludes (or, better, begins) with a new creation. The biblical Revelation 21:1 similarly announces a new heaven and a new earth. (In India the cyclical destruction of the universe is followed by a new creation of the world with its gods, humans, and creatures.)

In the renewed creation, a single god comes to govern: *þa kømr inn ríki at regindómi* ("then comes the Powerful One to ruling judgment"). In Iran it is stated—in almost literally identical terms—that Ohrmazd, the victorious principle of the good, will come into the renewed world (*Ohrmazd ō gētīg āyēd*). The Bible likewise speaks of the coming of the Son of Man in power and glory (Mark 13:26).

Christian Influence?

From the tenth century onward, Old Icelandic texts appear which depict the creation of the world and, most notably, the demise of the world. Foremost among these texts is the *Vǫluspá* and the literature that is connected to it.[†] A somewhat more recent eleventh-century runic inscription from Sweden (written at a time when the region was still heathen), which unmistakably echoes the wording of a verse about the end times in the *Vǫluspá,* suggests the proposition that here, at least, traditional conceptions were current—conceptions of which the Old Icelandic *Vǫluspá* also made use (presuming that the *Vǫluspá* itself could not already have been known in central Sweden at that time). The Swedish runic text reads: *iarþ s(k)al rifna uk ubhimin* (earth and heaven will burst).[7] In the southern Germanic realm, the theme of world destruction is found only in explicitly Christian texts, such as the Old Saxon

---

*[These two last survivors are appropriately named Líf (meaning "life") and Lífþrasir (meaning "life striver"). —*Trans.*]

†In the southern Germanic realm, Germanic creation mythology is found only in places where it has already been incorporated into Christian poetry ("Cædmon's Hymn," the "Wessobrunn Prayer").

Heliand and the Old High German "Muspilli," both of which date from the ninth century. The term that appears in connection with the biblical Last Judgment in these Continental texts[8]—variously spelled as *mutspelli, mudspelli,* or *muspilli* and apparently meaning "destruction of the world by fire, world in flames"—and the conceptions that relate to it could nevertheless be of heathen origin.

This raises a question: how is it possible that the Old Icelandic heathen scenario of the end times can be overtly consistent with the scenario from the Bible (apart from the idea of a Last Judgment according to a person's works, which is lacking in the Old Icelandic account) as well as with the scenario found in the Iranian (and Indian) cultural sphere? The Norse beliefs regarding the Creation and the beginnings of time can be set aside here, because they are not suspected of Christian origin or influence, but they do help corroborate the following considerations. The answer to our question, then, must be that we are dealing with a common Indo-European substratum of eschatological conceptions and an Indo-European scenario of the end times, which expressed itself in the Germanic and Iranian (and Indian) spheres under their specific historical circumstances. In the course of the close cultural contact between the land of the Israelites and Persia (Palestine was part of the greater Persian empire for two hundred years), these same conceptions and this same scenario also became a component of the Jewish, and later the Christian, notions of the apocalypse. The similarities between northern Germanic and Christian eschatology thus likely unfolded from a *common* (Indo-European) *source,* rather than being *primarily* the product of Christian influence. It is certainly possible, however, that Christian influence played a *secondary* role. In addition, the warlike spirit of the Viking Age may have also exerted a vivid and graphic influence on the "dramaturgy" of the Old Icelandic *"Götterdämmerung."*

By recontextualizing the ancient eschatological mythic material about the destruction of this world, northern Germanic religious poetry was able to deal mythologically with the ascendency of a new age that was marked by new values and a new God: the triumphant and advancing Christian world. For us modern people, living in a world whose very existence has become fragile and fractured by foreseeable ecological and social catastrophes of incalculable dimensions, an existential gateway is also opened up to this type of mythology. It is at this exact point, too, that the distance between us and a "Germanic essence" (a distance which our original "attempt at an approximation" undertook to show) begins to melt away.

Notes

Translator's Introduction

1. Turville-Petre's book, the subtitle of which is *The Religion of Ancient Scandinavia,*
first appeared in 1964 (New York: Holt, Reinhart and Winston) and was subsequently reprinted in 1975 (Westport, Conn.: Greenwood Press). Davidson's works
on the subject include *Gods and Myths of Northern Europe* (Baltimore: Penguin,
1964), *Pagan Scandinavia* (London: Thames and Hudson, 1967), *Scandinavian
Mythology* (London: Hamlyn, 1969), *Myths and Symbols in Pagan Europe: Early
Scandinavian and Celtic Religions* (Manchester: Manchester University Press,
1988), and *The Lost Beliefs of Northern Europe* (London: Routledge, 1993). An
excellent and up-to-date overview of Norse myth and religion has recently been
published by Christopher Abram titled *Myths of the Pagan North: The Gods of the
Norsemen* (London: Continuum, 2011), but—like the aforementioned works—this
also focuses squarely on Scandinavia.

2, For a general introduction to this methodology, see Lyle Campbell, *Historical
Linguistics: An Introduction,* 2nd edition (Cambridge, Mass.: MIT Press, 2004),
chapter 5, and Hans Henrich Hock and Brian D. Joseph, *Language History,
Language Change, and Language Relationship: An Introduction to Historical and
Comparative Linguistics* (Berlin and New York: Mouton De Gruyter, 1996), chap-
ters 2, 16, and 18.

3. Vries's two-volume study originally appeared in 1935–1937; a significantly revised
and expanded edition was issued in 1956–1957. All subsequent reprints are of the
second edition. More than five decades later, it remains the standard comprehen-
sive work on Germanic religions. Rudolf Simek's book on the subject, *Religion und
Mythologie der Germanen,* was published in 2003 (Stuttgart: Theiss). Also published that same year was Bernhard Maier's *Die Religion der Germanen: Götter—
Mythen—Weltbild* (Munich: C. H. Beck).

Introduction

1. In this regard, see Lothar Kilian, *Zum Ursprung der Germanen* (Bonn: Habelt, 1988), who provides a good overview of the problem but whose views I do not, incidentally, share.

2. For a discussion of the metaphysical representation of the Germanic peoples in National Socialist ideology, see Hans-Peter Hasenfratz, "Die Religion Alfred Rosenbergs," *Numen* 36, fasc. 1 (June, 1989): 113–26.

3. Regarding the inscription, see the entry for "Harigast" in Rudolph Simek, *Dictionary of Northern Mythology* (Cambridge: D. S. Brewer, 1993), 132. For an opposing view, see Åke V. Ström, "Germanische Religion," *Die Religionen der Menschheit*, vol. 19:1 (Stuttgart: Kohlhammer, 1975), 86.

4. Regarding the preceding comments: the gold object bearing the inscription *gutaniowihailag* is probably an oath ring; for more on these objects, see the entry "Ring oath" in Simek, *Dictionary of Northern Mythology*, 266. For more on the *Matronae*, see p. 111. For more on "linen and lauch" and the story of the horse phallus, see pp. 4, 103, 123.

5. H. M. Smyser, "Ibn Faḍlān's Account of the Rūs, with Some Commentary and Some Allusions to *Beowulf*" in Jess B. Bessinger and Robert P. Creed, eds., *Franciplegius: Medieval and Linguistic Studies in Honor of Francis Peabody Magoun, Jr.* (New York: New York University Press, 1965), 95–119.

6. A. Zeki Validi Togan, *Ibn Faḍlān's Reisebericht* (Leipzig: Deutsche Morgenländische Gesellschaft, 1939). Togan provides the Arabic text with German translation and commentary.

7. For translations of the text with commentary, see Smyser, "Ibn Faḍlān's Account of the Rūs," and Heinz-Joachim Graf, *Orientalische Berichte des Mittelalters über die Germanen: Eine Quellensammlung* (Krefeld: Verlag Schnelldruck F. Thyssen, 1971).

8. Georg Jacob, *Iskenders Warägerfeldzug: Ein iranischer Heldensang des Mittelalters aus Niẓâmî's Iskendernâme* (Glückstadt: J. J. Augustin 1934), 9–10.

9. Klaus Bemmann, *Der Glaube der Ahnen: Die Religion der Deutschen, bevor sie Christen wurden* (Essen: Phaidon, 1990), 57, 122, 131–32; figs. 10, 36, and 37.

10. *Hávamál* 49; Carolyn Larrington, trans., *The Poetic Edda* (Oxford: Oxford University Press, 1996), 21; German translation in F. Niedner, and Gustav Neckel, eds. *Thule: Altnordische Dichtung und Prosa,* 24 vols. (Düsseldorf and Cologne: Wissenschaftliche Buchgesellschaft, 1963–1967 [1912–1930]), vol. 2, 130.

11. Howell D. Chickering, Jr., trans., *Beowulf: A Dual-language Edition* (New York: Anchor, 2006), lines 28a–42b; 47a–52b.

12. Smyser, "Ibn Faḍlān's Account of the Rūs," 106–114, especially 107 and 109.

13. Folke Ström, *On the Sacral Origin of the Germanic Death Penalties* (Lund: Håkan Ohlssons Boktryckeri, 1942), 193, 246.

14. Chickering, *Beowulf*, lines 3137a–65b.

15. Jesse L. Byock, trans., *The Saga of King Hrolf Kraki* (London: Penguin, 1998), 48–50. German: Ludwig Ettmüller, *Altnordischer Sagenschatz in neun Büchern* (Leipzig: Verlag von Friedrich Fleischer Ettmüller, 1870), 355–7. See also Chickering, *Beowulf*, lines 64a–78a.

16. Saxo Grammaticus, *The History of the Danes, Books I–IX*, Hilda Ellis Davidson and Peter Fisher, eds. and trans. (Woodbridge: Brewer, 1996), vol. 1, 54. German: Ettmüller, *Altnordischer Sagenschatz*, 59; H. Jantzen, trans., *Saxo Grammaticus: Die ersten neun Bücher der dänischen Geschichte* (Berlin: Verlag von Emil Felber, 1900), 89.

Chapter 1. A Brief History of the Germanic Tribes

1. See Ström, "Germanische Religion," 15–18; Johannes Haller and Heinrich Dannenbauer, *Der Eintritt der Germanen in die Geschichte*, 4th edition (Berlin: Walter De Gruyter, 1970); and Bruno Krüger, ed., *Die Germanen: Geschichte und Kultur der germanischen Stämme in Mitteleuropa*, 2 vols. (Darmstadt: Wissenschaftliche Buchgesellschaft, 1987–1988).

2. Hans-Peter Hasenfratz, "Germanische Religion," in Franz König and Heinz Waldenfels, eds. *Lexikon der Religionen* (Freiburg: Herder, 1987), 193b; Jan de Vries, *Altnordisches etymologisches Wörterbuch*, 2nd edition (Leiden: Brill, 1977), 568b.

3. Compare Siân Grønlie, *Íslendingabók, Kristni saga: The Book of the Icelanders, The Story of the Conversion* (London: Viking Society for Northern Research, 2006); Hermann Pálsson and Paul Edwards, trans., *The Book of Settlements: Landnámabók*, (Winnipeg: University of Manitoba Press, 1972). German: Niedner and Neckel, *Thule*, vol. 23. *Eiriks saga rauða* and *Grænlendinga saga* both appear in *The Sagas of Icelanders* (New York: Viking, 2001). German: *Thule*, vol. 13.

4. Jacob, *Iskandarnāma*, 9–10, 21, 36–37.

5. Smyser, "Ibn Faḍlān's Account of the Rūs," 107.

6. Hans-Peter Hasenfratz, "Krieg und Frieden bei den alten Germanen," in Gerhard Binder and Bernd Effe, eds., *Krieg und Frieden im Altertum* (Trier: Wissenschaftlicher Verlag, 1989), 204–16.

7. Valentin Gitermann, *Die Geschichte Russlands*, vol. 1 (Zurich: Büchergilde Gutenberg, 1944), 38–45.

8. Ettmüller, *Altnordischer Sagenschatz*, 294–95, 299

9. Chapter 2 of the *Vatnsdæla saga* in *The Sagas of Icelanders*, 189–90. German: Niedner and Neckel, *Thule*, vol. 10, 23–24.

10. Text (Matthew 6:9–13) from Wilhelm Streitberg, *Die Gotische Bibel* (Heidelberg: Winter, 1971), 7 (translation mine).

11. Grønlie, *Íslendingabók* and *Kristni saga*. German: Niedner and Neckel, *Thule*, vol. 23. See also *Njáls saga* and *Laxdœla saga* (both in *The Sagas of Icelanders*). German: translations of the sagas appear in Niedner and Neckel, *Thule*, vols. 4 and 6, respectively.

12. Otto Gschwantler and Knut Schäferdiek, "Bekehrung und Bekehrungsgeschichte," in *Reallexikon der Germanischen Altertumskunde*, 2nd edition (Berlin: Walter De Gruyter, 1976), vol. 2, 175–205.

13. Compare *Materialdienst* (of the Evangelische Zentralstelle für Weltanschauungsfragen) 54/4 (1991).

14. Sigrid Hunke, *Europas eigene Religion* (Bergisch-Gladbach: Bastei Lubbe, 1983).

15. Bemmann, *Der Glaube der Ahnen: Die Religion der Deutschen, bevor sie Christen wurden* (Essen: Phaidon, 1990).

Chapter 2. Society and Its Values (Sociography and Axiology)

1. Ström, "Germanische Religion," 206–11; Heinrich Brunner, *Deutsche Rechtsgeschichte*, 2nd edition (Leipzig: Duncker and Humblot, 1906), vol. 1, 133–50.

2. Ibid.

3. *Rígsþula* (Larrington, *The Poetic Edda*, 246–52). German: Niedner and Neckel, *Thule* 2, 112–20.

4. Hasenfratz, "Die Religion Alfred Rosenbergs," 121; Joachim C. Fest, *Hitler*, trans. Richard and Clara Winston (New York: Harcourt Brace Jovanovich, 1974), 678.

5. Saxo, *The History of the Danes*, vol. 1, 143. German: Ettmüller, *Altnordischer Sagenschatz*, 171; Jantzen, *Saxo Grammaticus*, 244–45.

6. *The Sagas of Icelanders*, 287–88. German: Niedner and Neckel, *Thule*, vol. 6, 43–45.

7. *The Sagas of Icelanders* 2001, 181–83. German: Kurt Schier, ed. and trans., *Die Saga von Egil* (Darmstadt: Wissenschaftliche Buchgesellschaft, 1962), 262–63.

8. *Gulaþingslǫg* (Laurence M. Larson, trans., *The Earliest Norwegian Laws: Being the Gulathing Law and the Frostathing Law* [New York: Columbia University Press, 1935], 83; German: Rudolph Meissner, ed. and trans., *Norwegisches Recht: Das Rechtsbuch des Gulathings* [Weimar: Böhlau, 1935], 55; text and German translation also in Ström, "Germanische Religion," 212).

9. *Hávamál* 126 (Larrington, *The Poetic Edda*, 32). German: Niedner and Neckel, *Thule*, vol. 2, 133–34.

10. Ström, "Germanische Religion," 207.

11. *Hrólfs saga kraka* (Byock, trans., *The Saga of King Hrolf Kraki* [London: Penguin, 1998], 47–49). See also Ettmüller, *Altnordischer Sagenschatz*, 368.

12. *Gesta Danorum* (Saxo, *The History of the Danes*, vol. 1, 205). German: Jantzen, *Saxo Grammaticus*, 345). Compare also, with reference to Tacitus, Hans-Peter Hasenfratz, "Krieg und Frieden bei den alten Germanen," 205.

13. Siegfried Gutenbrunner, *Historische Laut und Formenlehre des Altisländischen; zugleich eine Einführung in das Urnordische* (Heidelberg: Winter, 1951), 12, numbers 128 and 129.

14. *Hrólfs saga kraka* (Byock, *The Saga of King Hrolf Kraki*, 47–49). German: Ettmüller, *Altnordischer Sagenschatz*, 368.

15. *Ynglinga saga* (in Snorri Sturluson, *Heimskringla: History of the Kings of Norway*, trans. Lee M. Hollander [Austin: University of Texas Press, 1964], 44–45, and 18–19). German: Niedner and Neckel, *Thule*, vol. 14, 70–71, and 41.

16. Saxo, *Gesta Danorum* (Saxo, *The History of the Danes*, 171–72); *Gautreks saga* (Pálsson and Edwards, *Gautrek's Saga and Other Medieval Tales*, 38–41) and *Víkarsbálkr* (Lee M. Hollander, trans., *Old Norse Poems: The Most Important Non-Skaldic Verse Not Included in the Poetic Edda* [New York: Columbia University Press, 1936], 18–25). German: Ettmüller, *Altnordischer Sagenschatz*, 202–3, 401–3.

17. Saxo, *Gesta Danorum* (Saxo, *The History of the Danes*, vol. 1, 157–58); *Grottasǫngr* (Larrington, *The Poetic Edda*, 260–63); *Skáldskaparmál/Hattatal* (Sturluson, *Edda*, trans. Anthony Faulkes [London: Dent, 1987], 193; *Ynglinga saga* (Sturluson, *Heimskringla*, 13–14). German: Ettmüller, *Altnordischer Sagenschatz*, 188–90 and 237–41; Niedner and Neckel, *Thule*, vol. 1, 173–77; *Thule*, vol. 20, 195–96; and *Thule*, vol. 14, 35–37.

18. On the Frothi laws, compare Jantzen, *Saxo Grammaticus*, 242, note 1, and the above note 5.

19. See textual note at p. 17.

20. Saxo, *Gesta Danorum* (Saxo, *The History of the Danes*, vol. 1, 101, 221); *Hrólfs saga kraka* (Byock, *The Saga of King Hrolf Kraki*, 40); *Gautreks saga* and *Gjafa-Refs saga* (Hermann Pálsson and Paul Edwards, trans. *Gautrek's Saga and Other Medieval Tales* [London: University of London Press, 1968], 34, 37–38, 43); *Grettis saga* (Jesse L. Byock, trans., *Grettir's Saga* [New York: Oxford University Press, 2009], 34–44). German: Ettmüller, *Altnordischer Sagenschatz*, 121, 268; 348; 395; 405, 406–7; Hubert Seelow, ed. and trans., *Die Saga von Grettir*, 1st edition (Darmstadt: Wissenschaftliche Buchgesellschaft, 1974), 35–43.

21. Along with the citations in note 20, see also *Egils saga* (*The Sagas of Icelanders*, 62–63) and *Jómsvíkinga saga* (Hollander, *The Saga of the Jómsvíkings*, 73). German: Schier, *Die Saga von Egil*, 105–8; Niedner and Neckel, *Thule*, vol. 19, 411.

22. Compare *Laxdæla saga* (*The Sagas of Icelanders*, 297). German: Niedner and Neckel, *Thule*, vol. 6, 57.

23. Compare *Egils saga* (*The Sagas of Icelanders*, 59–61, 71, and 74–75; 95–107, 129, and 133–34). German: Schier, *Die Saga von Egil*, 109–110; 117, and 119–22; 152–71, 199, and 205–7.

24. *The Sagas of Icelanders*, 180–82. German: Schier, *Die Saga von Egil*, 260–61.

25. Saxo, *Gesta Danorum* (Saxo, *The History of the Danes*, vol. 1, 247–52). German: Ettmüller, *Altnordischer Sagenschatz*, 309–315.

26. Compare *Ynglinga saga* (Sturluson, *Heimskringla*, 13). German: Niedner and Neckel, *Thule*. vol. 14, 35.

27. Ettmüller, *Altnordischer Sagenschatz*, 392; Ström, "Germanische Religion," 213–14. Regarding traces in the southern Germanic realm, see Jacob Grimm, *Deutsche Rechtsalterthümer*, reprint of 4th edition (Darmstadt: Wissenschaftliche Buchgesellschaft, 1983), vol. 1, 671.

28. Pálsson and Edwards, *Gautrek's Saga*, 29–32. German: Ettmüller, *Altnordischer Sagenschatz*, 386–88.

29. See Hasenfratz, "Krieg und Frieden," especially 210–15 with the corresponding references.

30. Pálsson and Edwards, *Gautrek's Saga*, 25–32. German: Ettmüller, *Altnordischer Sagenschatz*, 387–90.

31. Byock, *Grettir's Saga*, 43–47. German: Niedner and Neckel, *Thule*, vol. 21, 49–51.

32. *Gulaþingslǫg* (Larson, *The Earliest Norwegian Laws*, 53). German: Meissner, *Norwegisches Recht*, 23. *Östgöta Laghbok* (Dieter Strauch, trans., *Das Ostgötenrecht* (*Östgötalagen*) [Cologne: Böhlau Verlag, 1971]), 48.

33. Compare *Ynglinga saga* (Sturluson, *Heimskringla*, 8). German: Niedner and Neckel, *Thule*, vol. 14, 29. *Lokasenna* (Larrington, *The Poetic Edda*, 90–91). German: Niedner and Neckel, *Thule*, vol. 2, 55–56).

34. *Skáldskaparmál* (Sturluson, *Edda*, 61). German: Niedner and Neckel, *Thule*, vol. 20, 120.

35. The story of Gebe-Ref forms a part of the *Gautreks saga* (Pálsson and Edwards, *Gautrek's Saga*, 43–53). German: Ettmüller, *Altnordischer Sagenschatz*, 405–15.

36. Compare also Gisela Völger and Karin von Welck, eds., *Männerbünde–Männerbande: Zur Rolle des Mannes im Kulturvergleich* (Cologne: Rautenstrauch-Joest-Museum, 1990), 2 vols.

37. Compare *Grettis saga* (Byock, *Grettir's Saga*, 55–64 and 113–14). German: Seelow, *Die Saga von Grettir*, 53–60 and 109–11).

38. Hasenfratz, "Die Religion Alfred Rosenbergs," 121.

39. *Germania*, chapter 14 (Tacitus, *The Agricola and the Germania*, 113). For the original Latin with German translation, see Tacitus, *Germania*, trans. and ed. Manfred Fuhrmann (Stuttgart: Reclam, 1972), 22–23.

40. Saxo, *Gesta Danorum* (Saxo, *The History of the Danes*, vol. I, 121). German: Jantzen, *Saxo Grammaticus*, 200.

41. For the quotations, see Hasenfratz, "Krieg und Frieden," 217 note 48.

42. Jesse L. Byock, trans., *The Saga of the Volsungs: The Norse Epic of Sigurd the Dragon*

Slayer (Berkeley: University of California Press, 1990), 38–47. German: Niedner and Neckel, *Thule*, vol. 21, 43–56.

43. Old High German text from Wilhelm Braune, *Althochdeutsches Lesebuch*, 14th edition (Tübingen: Niemeyer, 1965), 84, my translation.

44. *Šāhnāma* (Ferdowsi, *The Epic of the Kings*, trans. Reuben Levy [London: Routledge and Kegan Paul, 1967], 75–80). German: Werner and Dorothea Heiduczek, *Die schönsten Sagen aus Firdausis Königsbuch* (Hanau: Kinderbuch Verlag, 1982), 102*ff.*

45. On this, compare Ström, *On the Sacral Origin of the Germanic Death Penalties;* Hans-Peter Hasenfratz, *Die toten Lebenden: Eine religionsphänomenologische Studie zum sozialen Tod in archaischen Gesellschaften, zugleich ein kritischer Beitrag zur sogenannten Strafopfertheorie* (Leiden: Brill, 1982), 24, and the citations given there with further literary references.

46. Compare Schier, *Die Saga von Egil,* 297.

47. Compare *Njals saga* (Robert Cook, trans., *Njal's Saga,* London: Penguin, 2001). German: Niedner and Neckel, *Thule,* vol. 4. The saga also shows the influence of Christianity: the two who remain alive from the feuding parties reconcile with one another and the slaughter is brought to an end.

48. We may compare the fateful roles of Hallgerd and Bergthora in *Njals saga* (above note 47) or the ill-fated Yngvild Faircheek in the *Svarfdœla saga* (*The Complete Sagas of Icelanders,* vol. 4, 181). German: Niedner and Neckel, *Thule,* vol. 11, 279.

49. *The Complete Sagas of Icelanders* 1997, vol. V, 313–47. German: Niedner and Neckel, *Thule,* vol. 8, 135–88.

50. *Germania,* chapter 19 (Tacitus, *The Agricola and the Germania,* 117). For the original Latin with German trans., see Publius Cornelius Tacitus, *Germania,* ed. and trans. Eugen Fehrle and Richard Hünnerkopf, 5th edition (Heidelberg: Winter, 1959), 34–35, commentary on 103–4.

51. The report is recounted in Hermann Schreiber, *Die Zehn Gebote: Der Mensch und sein Recht,* 1st edition (Vienna and Düsseldorf: Econ-Verlag, 1962), 192–93.

52. Compare *Helgaviða Hundingsbana II* (Larrrington, *The Poetic Edda,* 132–41). German: Niedner and Neckel, *Thule,* vol. 1, 142–52).

53. *Tryggðamál* (Hasenfratz, *Die toten Lebenden,* 14, my translation; for English, see Andrew Dennis, Peter Foote, and Richard Perkins, trans., *Laws of Early Iceland: Grágás I* [Winnipeg: University of Manitoba Press, 1980], 184–85; for German in context, see Niedner and Neckel, *Thule,* vol. 2, 189–90); *Grettis saga* (Byock, *Grettir's Saga,* 192; German: Seelow, *Die Saga von Grettir,* 183, note 237).

54. *Wulf and Eadwacer* (Hasenfratz, *Die toten Lebenden,* 51–52: my translation). The Old English text appears in George P. Krapp and Elliot Van Kirk Dobbie, eds., *The*

Exeter Book (New York: Columbia University Press, 1936), 179–80. German: Rolf Breuer and Rainer Schöwerling, eds., *Altenglische Lyrik* (Stuttgart: Reclam 1972), 38–39.

55. *Germania,* chapter 12 (Tacitus, *The Agricola and the Germania,* 111, with the phrase rendered here as "cowards, shirkers, and sodomites"). For original Latin with German trans., see Tacitus, *Germania* (1959), 26–29, and Tacitus, *Germania* (1972), 20–21.

56. Ström, *On the Sacral Origin of the Germanic Death Penalties,* 178.

57. Hasenfratz, *Die toten Lebenden,* 128, note 88 (relating to Dätgen), 23–24; 107, note 117; 146, note 236 (relating to bog corpse finds in the region of northern Europe).

58. *Germania,* chapter 12 (Tacitus, *The Agricola and the Germania,* 1970, 111). For original Latin with German trans., see Tacitus, *Germania* (1959), 26–27.

59. Saxo, *Gesta Danorum* (Saxo, *The History of the Danes,* vol. I, 152). German: Jantzen, *Saxo Grammaticus,* 263.

60. Hans-Peter Hasenfratz, "Der indogermanische 'Männerbund': Anmerkungen zur religiösen und sozialen Bedeutung des Jugendalters," in *Zeitschrift für Religions und Geistesgeschichte* 34, no. 2 (1982): 159–60; Hasenfratz, *Die toten Lebenden,* 146, note 227.

Chapter 3. The Rituals of Transition (Rites of Passage)

1. In this regard, see Grimm, *Deutsche Rechtsalterthümer,* vol. I, 627–41. See also Vilhelm Grönbech, *The Culture of the Teutons* (London: Oxford University Press, 1932), vol. II, 42–53; Hasenfratz, *Die toten Lebenden,* 3–4, 81–82; and Hans-Peter Hasenfratz, "Seelenvorstellungen bei den Germanen und ihre Übernahme und Umformung durch die christliche Mission," *Zeitschrift für Religions- und Geistesgeschichte* 38, no. 1 (1982), 22; and Hans-Peter Hasenfratz, *Die Seele: Einführung in ein religiöses Grundphänomen* (Zürich: Theologischer Verlag, 1986), 83–84.

2. *Vatnsdœla saga* (*The Sagas of Icelanders,* 193). German: Niedner and Neckel, *Thule,* vol. 10, 28.

3. *The Complete Sagas of Icelanders,* vol. II, 200. See also Niedner and Neckel, *Thule,* vol. 8, 200. Regarding Tacitus, see Tacitus, *Germania* (1972), 79.

4. Compare the thirteenth-century *Östgöta Laghbok* (Strauch, *Das Ostgötenrecht,* 54, 66).

5. Hasenfratz, *Die toten Lebenden,* 29–30 and 114–15, note 184, 53 and 135–36, also 108, note 130.

6. *Rúnatal þáttr Óðins* section of the *Hávamál* (Larrington, *The Poetic Edda,* 29, 34). German: Niedner and Neckel, *Thule,* vol. 2, 171–72.

7. Compare *Ynglinga saga* (Sturluson, *Heimskringla,* 10); *Hrólfs saga kraka* (Byock,

The Saga of King Hrolf Kraki, 73–76). German: Niedner and Neckel, *Thule*, vol. 14, 32; Ettmüller, *Altnordischer Sagenschatz*, 378–79.

8. *Þrymskviða* (Larrington, *The Poetic Edda*, 97–101). German: Niedner and Neckel, *Thule*, vol. 2, 11–16.

9. Brunner, *Deutsche Rechtsgeschichte*, 39, 101.

10. *The Sagas of Icelanders*, 277. German: Niedner and Neckel, *Thule*, vol. 6, 83.

11. *Laxdæla saga* (*The Sagas of Icelanders*, 277 and 279). German: Niedner and Neckel, *Thule*, vol. 6, 29 and 32).

12. *Egils saga* (*The Sagas of Icelanders*, 46–47). German: *Die Saga von Egil*, 76–80.

13. On this and the following, see Schier, *Die Saga von Egil*, 312.

14. *Sigrdrífumál* 34 (Larrington, *The Poetic Edda*, 171). German: Niedner and Neckel, *Thule*, vol. 2, 141.

15. Compare Ström, "Germanische Religion," 190–91.

16. *Eyrbyggja saga* (Paul Schach, and Lee M. Hollander, trans., *Eyrbyggja Saga* [Lincoln: University of Nebraska Press, 1959], 69–70); *Hávarðar saga* (*The Complete Sagas of Icelanders*, vol. V, 316–19); *Svarfdæla saga* (*The Complete Sagas of Icelanders*, vol. IV, 173). German: Niedner and Neckel, *Thule*, vol. 7, 86; *Thule*, vol. 8, 141–45; *Thule*, vol. 11, 267–68.

17. Compare Hans and Ida Naumann, trans., *Isländische Volksmärchen* (Jena: Diederichs, 1923), 51–54.

18. *Helgaviða Hundingsbana II*, 45 (Larrington, *The Poetic Edda*, 140). German: Niedner and Neckel, *Thule*, vol. 1, 160. Compare the fairy-tale motifs of the "little shirt of death" and the "cup of tears."

19. *Grettis saga* (Byock, *The Saga of the Volsungs*, 94). German: Seelow, *Die Saga von Grettir*, 92.

20. Tacitus, *Germania* (Tacitus, *The Agricola and the Germania*, 111, with the translation "wicker hurdle"). Original Latin with German trans.: Tacitus, *Germania* (1959), 28–29.

21. *The Sagas of Icelanders*, 664. German: Niedner and Neckel, *Thule*, vol. 13, 15.

22. See Ström, "Germanische Religion," 181–94 (for the northern Germanic area).

23. See *Njáls saga* (Cook, *Njal's Saga*, 130). German: Niedner and Neckel, *Thule*, vol. 4, 171–72.

24. *Grettis saga* (Byock, *Grettir's Saga*, 50–53 and 91–103); *Laxdæla saga* (*The Sagas of Icelanders*, 297–98 and 317); *Eyrbyggja saga* (Schach and Hollander, *Eyrbyggja Saga*, 69–71 and 131–32, 108–11); *Svarfdæla saga* (*The Complete Sagas of Icelanders*, vol. IV, 176–77). German: Seelow, *Die Saga von Grettir*, 50–52 and 91–100; Niedner and Neckel, *Thule*, vol. 6, 57–58 and 84–85; *Thule*, vol. 7, 85–88 and 152–54, 128–31; Niedner and Neckel, *Thule*, vol. 11, 272–73.

25. Hasenfratz, *Die toten Lebenden*, 18–19.

26. *Eyrbyggja saga* (Schach and Hollander, *Eyrbyggja Saga*, 6). German: Niedner and Neckel, *Thule*, vol. 7, 19–20.

27. Fest, *Hitler*, 521 and 513–14.

28. Hans-Peter Hasenfratz, "Seelenvorstellungen bei den Germanen und ihre Übernahme und Umformung durch die christliche Mission," *Zeitschrift für Religions- und Geistesgeschichte* 38, no. 1 (1982), 19–31, 28–9, 30. See also Hasenfratz, *Die Seele*, 89–91.

29. See Hasenfratz, *Die toten Lebenden*, 21–23.

30. *Grímnismál* (Larrington, *The Poetic Edda*, 52–55) and *Gylfaginning* (Sturluson, *Edda*, 24, 31–34, 55–56). German: Niedner and Neckel, *Thule*, vol. 2, 82–83 [and following]; *Thule*, vol. 20, 82, and 84–87, 73).

31. *Helgaviða Hundingsbana II* (Larrington, *The Poetic Edda*, 132–41). German: Niedner and Neckel, *Thule*, vol. 1, 142–52.

32. As in the references given in note 24 above.

33. On this and the following, see Hasenfratz, *Die Seele*, 49–50 and 119 (with references).

34. *Egils saga* (*The Sagas of Icelanders*, 151). German: Schier, *Die Saga von Grettir*, 232.

Chapter 4. Magic

1. Regarding this phenomenon, see Paul Hermann, *Das altgermanische Priesterwesen* (Jena: Diederichs, 1929), 16–21.

2. *Wið Dweorh* (original Old English in George P. Krapp and Elliot Van Kirk Dobbie, *The Anglo-Saxon Minor Poems* [New York: Columbia University Press, 1942], 121–22). German: Breuer and Schöwerling, *Altenglische Lyrik*, 56, 57, and 149–52. In general, I have followed the translation of the German editors.

3. Compare Hasenfratz, *Die Seele,* 21 and 114, note 12.

4. See Klaus Düwel, "Buchstabenmagie und Alphabetzauber: Zu den Inschriften der Goldbrakteaten und ihrer Function als Amulette," *Früh Mittelalterliche Studien* 22 (1988), 101–10.

5. Klaus Düwel and Michael Gebühr, "Die Fibel von Meldorf und die Anfänge der Runenschrift," *Zeitschrift für Deutsches Altertum und deutsche Literatur* 110 (1981): 159–77.

6. Tacitus, *The Agricola and the Germania*, 109–110. For original Latin with German trans., see Tacitus, *Germania* (1959) 24–5, 90–93, and Tacitus, *Germania* (1972), 16–17, 74.

7. Compare Vries, *Altnordisches etymologisches Wörterbuch*, 7.

8. The Norse runic inscriptions with *alu-* and *laukaʀ-* are readily accessible and appear with German translations in Gutenbrunner, *Historische Laut- und Formenlehre des*

Altisländischen, 8–16 (nos. 4, 9, 108, 109, 112, and 124). On the topic of encipherment, see Düwel, "Buchstabenmagie und Alphabetzauber" (full citation above at note 4).

9. *Vegtamskviða* (Larrington, *The Poetic Edda,* 243). German: Niedner and Neckel, *Thule,* vol. 2, 25.

10. *Hervararkviða* [i.e., "The Waking of Angantyr"] (Patricia Terry, trans., *Poems of the Elder Edda,* revised edition [Philadelphia: University of Pennsylvania Press, 1990], 248–53). German: Niedner and Neckel, *Thule,* vol. 1, 212.

11. *Grógaldr* (Henry Adams Bellows, trans., *The Poetic Edda* [New York: American-Scandinavian Foundation, 1923], 234–51). German: Niedner and Neckel, *Thule,* vol. 2, 178.

12. *Gesta Danorum* (Saxo, *The History of the Danes,* vol. I, 23). German: Jantzen, *Saxo Grammaticus,* 32–3 and 33, note 1.

13. Düwel, "Buchstabenmagie und Alphabetzauber," 75, 77, 90, 105.

14. Wilhelm Boudriot, *Die altgermanische Religion in der amtlichen kirchlichen Literatur des Abendlandes vom 5. bis 11. Jahrhundert* (Bonn: Ludwig Röhrscheid Verlag, 1964), 51.

15. *Eiríks saga rauða* (*The Sagas of Icelanders,* 658–59); *Hrólfs saga kraka* (Byock, *The Saga of King Hrolf Kraki,* 6–7). German: Niedner and Neckel, *Thule.* vol. 13, 28–50; Ettmüller, *Altnordischer Sagenschatz,* 321–22.

16. Saxo, *Gesta Danorum* (Saxo, *The History of the Danes,* vol. I, 128); *Egils saga* (*The Sagas of Icelanders,* 106–107). German: Jantzen, *Saxo Grammaticus,* 214; Schier, *Die Saga von Egil,* 170.

17. Compare Walther Steller, "Pferdekopf," in *Handwörterbuch des deutschen Aberglaubens* (Berlin and New York: Walter De Gruyter, 1987), vol. 6, 1664–70.

18. Byock, *Grettir's Saga,* 201–209. German: Seelow, *Die Saga von Grettir,* 196–201.

19. On this see Boudriot, *Die altgermanische Religion,* 7, 20, 24. The name also comes from him.

20. Latin text in Boudriot, *Die altgermanische Religion,* 47 (nos. 176 and 173: love magic), 42 (no. 194: rain magic). The translation is mine.

21. Contrary to Boudriot, I read *inquietae noctis silentio* here (as does Migne). [Jacques Paul Migne (1800–1875) was a French theologian who published numerous editions of church documents, including the penitentials under discussion here. –*Trans.*]

22. Compare *Laxdæla saga* (*The Sagas of Icelanders,* 368, 373). German: Niedner and Neckel, *Thule,* vol. 6, 156, 162.

23. Compare Heinrich Marzell, "Bilsenkraut," in *Handwörterbuch des Deutschen Aberglaubens,* 1st edition (Berlin and New York: Walter De Gruyter, 1987), 1306–7.

24. This is from the so-called Anglo-Saxon Field Blessing (Ström, "Germanische Religion," 107; Old English text in Krapp and Dobbie, *The Anglo-Saxon Minor Poems,* 116–18, under the title "[Metrical Charm] For Unfruitful Land").

Chapter 5. The Powers

1. In this regard, see Hasenfratz, "Seelenvorstellungen bei den Germanen," 20–31; Hasenfratz, *Die Seele,* 82–93 and 20–26, with the relevant sources and examples. Regarding paragraph 1, see Naumann, *Isländische Volksmärchen,* 259–60 and 313 (with the note to fairy tale 64).

2. Animal shapeshifting of warriors: *Herrauðs saga ok Bósa* (Pálsson and Edwards, *Gautrek's Saga,* 86); *Svarfdœla saga* (*The Complete Sagas of Icelanders,* vol. IV, 177). German: Ettmüller, *Altnordischer Sagenschatz,* 468; Niedner and Neckel, *Thule,* vol. 1, 273.

3. The earliest attestation in the Germanic sphere is found in the so-called *Deutsches Bußbuch* (German Penitential). See also Boudriot, *Die altgermanische Religion,* 52–53 (no. 151).

4. For a detailed discussion, see Wolfgang Golther, *Handbuch der germanischen Mythologie,* reprint of 2nd edition (Kettwig: Magnus-Verlag, 1985), 122–58, and especially Grimm, *Teutonic Mythology,* vol. 2, 439–557.

5. Compare Grimm's German Legends [*Deutsche Sagen*] and Grimm's Fairy Tales [*Kinder- und Hausmärchen*]; and see also Heinrich Heine's witty essay about the "Elementargeister" (elemental spirits). With regard to the northern regions, see Naumann, *Isländische Volksmärchen;* Benjamin Thorpe, *Northern Mythology: From Pagan Faith to Local Legends* (Ware, Hertfordshire: Wordsworth Editions, 2001), part 2; and Jacqueline Simpson, *Icelandic Folktales and Legends* (Berkeley: University of California Press, 1972).

6. Ström, "Germanische Religion," 163–75.

7. Compare *Helgakviða Hjǫrvarðssonar* (Larrington, *The Poetic Edda,* 123–31). German: Niedner and Neckel, *Thule,* vol. 1, 161–72.

8. *Grettis saga* (Byock, trans., *Grettir's Saga,* 91–93). German: Seelow, *Die Saga von Grettir,* 89–92.

9. Compare Hans Vordemfelde, *Die germanische Religion in den deutschen Volksrechten; Erster Halbband: Der religiöse Glaube* (Giessen: Verlag von Alfred Töpelmann, 1923), 62–111; Boudriot, *Die altgermanische Religion,* 24–46; Grimm, *Teutonic Mythology,* vol. 1, 101–4, and vol. 2, 582–697.

10. See Ström, "Germanische Religion," 113–63 (on the northern Germanic peoples); Jakob Amstadt, *Südgermanische Religion seit der Völkerwanderungszeit* (Stuttgart: W. Kohlhammer, 1991), 37–46 (southern Germanic peoples); and the relevant entries in Simek, *Dictionary of Northern Mythology.*

11. The most important sources are *Vǫluspá*; *Gylfaginning, Grímnismál*; *Vafþrúðnismál* (see Larrington, *The Poetic Edda*, [for *Vǫluspá, Grímnismál*, and *Vafþrúðnismál*] and Sturluson, *Edda*, [for *Gylfaginning*]). German: Franz Rolf Schröder, *Die Germanen*, 2nd edition (Tübingen: Mohr, 1929), 48–54; 43–44 and 47–48; 55. Regarding *Vǫluspá*, see the commentary of Sigurður Nordal, ed., *Völuspá. Aus dem Isländischen übersetzt und mit einem Vorwort zur deutschen Ausgabe von Ommo Wilts* (Darmstadt: Wissenschaftliche Buchgesellschaft, 1980), 25–116.

12. On the weekday names, which have no connection to the conversion to Christianity, see Adolf Bach, *Geschichte der deutschen Sprache*, 6th edition (Heidelberg: Quelle and Meyer, 1956), 69–70.

13. Saxo, *Gesta Danorum* (Saxo, *The History of the Danes*, vol. I, 226–27 [and see corresponding notes and diagram in vol. 2], 31). German: Jantzen, *Saxo Grammaticus*, 386–89, illustration of the formation on 387; 48–49.

14. Saxo, *Gesta Danorum* (Saxo, *The History of the Danes*, vol. I, 228 and 232–44). German: Jantzen, *Saxo Grammaticus*, 391 and 398–412; Ettmüller, *Altnordischer Sagenschatz*, 279 and 285–306.

15. Hasenfratz, "Krieg und Frieden," 209 and 216, note 19.

16. Hasenfratz, "Der indogermanische 'Männerbund,'" 158.

17. *Ynglinga saga* (Sturluson, *Heimskringla: History of the Kings of Norway*, 10–11). German: Niedner and Neckel, *Thule*, vol. 14, 31–33.

18. *Gylfaginning* and *Hávamál* (see Sturluson, *Heimskringla: History of the Kings of Norway*, for the former; Larrington, *The Poetic Edda*, for the latter). German: Schröder, *Die Germanen*, 4–7.

19. Saxo, *Gesta Danorum* (Saxo, *The History of the Danes*, vol. 1, 76–78). German: Jantzen, *Saxo Grammaticus*, 124–29.

20. Compare *Vǫlsunga saga* (Byock, *The Saga of the Volsungs*, 38). German: Niedner and Neckel, *Thule*, vol. 21, 43 with note 2.

21. See Simek, *Dictionary of Northern Mythology*, 313.

22. *Gylfaginning* (Sturluson, *Edda*, 27–29). German: Niedner and Neckel, *Thule*, vol. 20, 76–80.

23. *Ólafs saga Tryggvasonar* (Oddr Snorrason, *The Saga of Olaf Tryggvason*, trans. Theodore M. Andersson (Ithaca, N.Y.: Cornell University Press, 2003), 108. German: Schröder, *Die Germanen*, 73.

24. *Gylfaginning* (Sturluson, *Edda*, 37–38). German: Niedner and Neckel, *Thule*, vol. 20, 91–92.

25. See the entry "Thor's goats" in Simek, *Dictionary of Northern Mythology*, 325. See also Bemmann, *Der Glaube der Ahnen*, 131–32.

26. See Hans-Peter Hasenfratz, "Iran und der Dualismus," *Numen* 30, vol. 30, fasc. 1 (July, 1983), 43–44 and 50–51, note 69 and following.

27. Compare the entry "Fricco" in Simek, *Dictionary of Northern Mythology,* 93. See also Jan de Vries, *Altgermanische Religionsgeschichte,* 3rd edition (Berlin: Walter De Gruyter, 1970), vol. II, 188, note 3.

28. Adam von Bremen, *Gesta Hammaburgensis ecclesiae pontificum* (Francis J. Tschan, trans., *The History of the Archbishops of Hamburg-Bremen by Adam of Bremen* [New York: Columbia University Press, 2002], 207–08); Saxo, *Gesta Danorum* (Saxo, *The History of the Danes,* vol. I, 73, 172). German: Schröder, *Die Germanen,* 61–62; Jantzen, *Saxo Grammaticus,* 119, 297.

29. *Skírnismál* (Larrington, *The Poetic Edda,* 61–68) and *Vǫluspá in skamma* (Bellows, *The Poetic Edda,* 228). German: Niedner and Neckel, *Thule,* vol. 2, 27–33, 45.

30. *Gunnars þattr Helmings* (John McKinnell, trans. *Viga-Glums Saga, With the Tales of Ögmund Bash and Thorvald Chatterbox* [Edinburgh: Canongate/UNESCO, 1987], 141–44). German: Schröder, *Die Germanen,* 24–27.

31. *Vǫlsa þáttr* (Original Old Icelandic text with notes and commentary in English appears in Anthony Faulkes, ed., *Stories from the Sagas of the Kings* [London: Viking Society for Northern Research, 1980], 50–61). German: Niedner and Neckel, *Thule,* vol. 2, 184–88). On this, see the entry "Vǫlsi" in Simek, *Dictionary of Northern Mythology,* 365–66.

32. *Skáldskarparmál* and *Gylfaginning* (Sturluson, *Edda,* 61; 23–24). German: Niedner and Neckel, *Thule,* vol. 20, 119; 71–72.

33. *Gylfaginning* (Sturluson, *Edda,* 26). German: Niedner and Neckel, *Thule,* vol. 20, 76.

34. *Gylfaginning* (Sturluson, *Edda,* 72). German: Niedner and Neckel, *Thule,* vol. 20, 103.

35. *Gylfaginning* (Sturluson, *Edda,* 26–29). German: Niedner and Neckel, *Thule,* vol. 20, 76–80.

36. *Gylfaginning* (Sturluson, *Edda,* 48–52). German: Niedner and Neckel, *Thule,* vol. 20, 103–8. Compare also the (old?) Eddic poem *Vegtamskviða* [*Baldrs Draumar*] (Larrington, *The Poetic Edda,* 243–44). German: Niedner and Neckel, *Thule,* vol. 2, 24–26.

37. See the entry "Second Merseburg Charm" in Simek, *Dictionary of Northern Mythology,* 278–79, which includes the Old High German text and a translation.

38. Ettmüller, *Altnordischer Sagenschatz,* 95, note 21.

39. *Gesta Danorum* (Saxo, *The History of the Danes,* vol. 1, 69–76). German: Jantzen, *Saxo Grammaticus,* 109–24.

40. Compare *Bahman Yašt* (Geo Widengren, *Iranische Geisteswelt: Von den Anfängen bis zum Islam,* 207–8) and Firdausī, *Šāhnāma* (Heiduczek, *Die schönsten Sagen aus Firdausis Königsbuch,* 9, 17, and the miniature on 6).

41. Saxo, *Gesta Danorum* (Saxo, *The History of the Danes,* vol. 1, 267–70); *Gylfaginning*

(Sturluson, *Edda*, 40–46). German: Jantzen, *Saxo Grammaticus*, 455–62: Ugarthilocus; Niedner and Neckel, *Thule*, vol. 20, 92–103. The latter source parallels Naumann, *Isländische Volksmärchen*, 2–11.

42. Compare *Saeculum* 34, issues 3–4 (1983): the double issue is entirely devoted to the theme "Gott–Gegengott" (God–Antigod).

43. Saxo Grammaticus, *Gesta Danorum* (Saxo, *The History of the Danes* vol. 1, 25–26), and *Lokasenna* (Larrington, *The Poetic Edda*, 89). German: Schröder, *Die Germanen*, 7–8; 39.

44. *Lokasenna* (Larrington, *The Poetic Edda*, 90). German: Schröder, *Die Germanen*, 40.

45. *Ynglinga saga* (Sturluson, *Heimskringla*, 8). German: Niedner and Neckel, *Thule*, vol. 14, 29.

46. *Sǫrla þáttr* (Georges Dumézil, *Loki* [Darmstadt: Wissenschaftliche Buchgesellschaft, 1959], 27; Ström, "Germanische Religion," 129).

47. Vries, *Altnordisches etymologisches Wörterbuch*, 283.

48. *Vǫlsunga saga* (George K. Anderson, trans., *The Saga of the Völsungs, Together with Excerpts from the* Nornagestsstháttr *and Three Chapters from the Prose Edda* [Newark: University of Delaware Press, 1982], 57–58). German: Niedner and Neckel, *Thule*, vol. 21, 41. [A recent translation differs slightly here, with the man eating the apple, but the fertility-increasing property of the fruit remains. Compare Jesse L. Byock, trans., *The Saga of the Volsungs: The Norse Epic of Sigurd the Dragon Slayer*. (Berkeley: University of California Press, 1990), 36–37, with the corresponding note 13. —*Trans.*]

49. *Gylfaginning* and *Skáldskaparmál* (Sturluson, *Edda*, 25; 59–60). German: Niedner and Neckel, *Thule*, vol. 20, 74 and 117–19.

50. Compare Vries, *Altnordisches etymologisches Wörterbuch*, 411a.

51. *Germania* (Tacitus, *The Agricola and the Germania*, 135). For original Latin with German trans., see Tacitus, *Germania* (1972), 54–57; Tacitus, *Germania* (1959), 52–53.

52. Georg Müller, *Zeugnisse germanischer Religion, Kirche und Erziehung* (Munich: Kaiser, 1935), 158.

53. *Germania* (Tacitus, *The Agricola and the Germania*, 137, with the name appearing as "Alci"). For original Latin with German trans., see Tacitus, *Germania*, 54–57, and in this regard 128–29.

54. Recent research is offered by the contributions that appear Gerhard Bauchhenss and Günter Neumann, eds., *Matronen und verwandte Gottheiten: Ergebnisse eines Kolloquiums veranstaltet von der Göttinger Akademiekommission für die Altertumskunde Mittel- und Nordeuropas* (Cologne and Bonn: Rheinland Verlag/ Habelt, 1987). The texts most relevant to our discussion are those by Horn, Neumann, and Petrikovits.

55. See Bauchhenss and Neumann, *Matronen und verwandte Gottheiten*, table 2.

56. Günter Neumann, "Die germanischen Matronen Beinamen," in Bauchhenss and Neumann, *Matronen und verwandte Gottheiten*, 114–15. A different assessment (with *Aufaniae* being the second-most-frequent name on inscriptions) is in the entry for "Matron names" in Simek, *Dictionary of Northern Mythology*, 207–8.

57. Ludwig Bechstein, "Von dem altfränkischen Götzen Lollus," *Der Sagenschatz des Frankenlandes, Erster Teil* (Würzburg: Voigt and Mocker, 1842), 25–26. See also Amstadt, *Südgermanische Religion*, 147 (illustration).

58. Amstadt, *Südgermanische Religion*, 47, 56, 76, 121–24. I am expressing Amstadt's hypotheses here.

59. *Vegtamskviða [Baldrs Daumar]* (Larrington, *The Poetic Edda*, 243–45). German: Niedner and Neckel, *Thule*, vol. 2, 24–26.

60. Fritz Genzmer, trans., *Beowulf und das Finnsburg-Bruchstück* (Stuttgart: Reclam, 1975), 77. [For modern English trans., see Chickering, *Beowulf,* 200–201, specifically, lines 2526–27. Chickering translates *metod* as "Lord," (that is, the Christian God) which the word came to mean; this is a semantic development which Hasenfratz discusses at the end of the section. —*Trans.*]

61. *Gylfaginning* (Sturluson, *Edda,* 18); *Vǫluspá* (Larrington, *The Poetic Edda,* 6). German: Niedner and Neckel, *Thule,* vol. 20, 64; Schröder, *Die Germanen,* 49.

62. Saxo, *Gesta Danorum* (Saxo, *The History of the Danes,* vol. 1, 169); *Nornagests Þáttr* (Anderson, *The Saga of the Völsungs,* 186–87). German: Jantzen, *Saxo Grammaticus,* 289–90; Ettmüller, *Altnordischer Sagenschatz,* 200, 95, note 20; Niedner and Neckel, *Thule,* vol. 21, 216–18. The motif of the hero Meleager is additionally present here.

63. See the Saxo citation in the preceding note.

64. Compare Nordal, *Völuspá,* 39.

65. *Cædmon's Hymn* (Old English text in Krapp and Dobbie, *The Anglo-Saxon Minor Poems,* 105). German: Breuer and Schöwerling, *Altenglische Lyrik,* 60, 61, and 154.

66. Contra Ström, "Germanische Religion," 255–60.

67. Compare the entries for *"álfablót"* and *"dísablót"* in Simek, *Dictionary of Northern Mythology,* 7–8 and 60–61, respectively.

68. *Hálfdanar saga svarta* (Sturluson, *Heimskringla,* 58). German: Schröder, *Die Germanen,* 63. On the remnants of Germanic royal worship, see Vordemfelde, *Die germanische Religion,* 121–23.

69. *Landnámabók* (Rev. T. Ellwood, *The Book of the Settlement of Iceland, Translated from the Original Icelandic of Ari the Learned* [Kenal: T. Wilson, 1898], 176–77). German: Niedner and Neckel, *Thule,* vol. 23, 134.

70. *Egils saga* (*The Sagas of Icelanders,* 106–7). German: Schier, *Die Saga von Egil,* 106–7.

71. See the reference in note 7 above.

72. Larrington, *The Poetic Edda,* 128 [with *helstafir* translated rather freely as "fatal runes"]. German: Niedner and Neckel, *Thule,* vol. 1, 179.

73. Compare the entry "Water" in Simek, *Dictionary of Northern Mythology,* 371.

74. See the literature cited in note 9 above, along with the accompanying "supporting documents."

75. Hasenfratz, *Die toten Lebenden,* 63 and 147–48, note 240 and note 241 (document). For the north, see *Jómsvíkinga saga,* in which a jarl sacrifices his seven-year-old son to two local weather goddesses for assistance (Lee M. Hollander, trans., *The Saga of the Jómsvíkings* [Austin: University of Texas Press, 1990], 100). German: Niedner and Neckel, *Thule,* vol. 19, 427.

76. Bemmann, *Der Glaube der Ahnen,* 130–31, and figs. 33 and 34 (pp. 120–21).

77. Hasenfratz, "Krieg und Frieden," 208.

78. *Orkneyinga saga* (Pálsson and Edwards, trans., *Orkneyinga saga: The History of the Earls of Orkney* [London: Hogarth, 1978], 33–34). German: Niedner and Neckel, *Thule,* vol. 19, 27.

79. *Gautreks saga* (Pálsson and Edwards, *Gautrek's Saga,* 40). German: Ettmüller, *Altnordischer Sagenschatz,* 403.

80. Compare *Helgakviða Hjǫrvarðssonar* (Larrington, *The Poetic Edda,* 129). German: Niedner and Neckel, *Thule,* vol. 1, 180.

81. Compare Bemmann, *Der Glaube der Ahnen,* 130–34.

82. Schach and Hollander, *Eyrbyggja Saga,* 4–6. German: Schröder, *Die Germanen,* 59–60; Niedner and Neckel, *Thule,* vol. 7, 18–19.

83. This "sacrificial feast" features in the title of Klaus Düwel, *Das Opferfest von Lade: Quellenkritische Untersuchungen zur germanischen Religionsgeschichte* (Vienna: Halosar, 1985), which critically investigates the Nordic and continental literary sources for heathen sacrificial ceremonies. See *Hákonar saga góða* (Sturluson, *Heimskringla,* 107). German: Niedner and Neckel, *Thule,* vol. 14, 149–50.

84. Compare also the entry "Sacrifices" in Simek, *Dictionary of Northern Mythology,* 271–73.

85. Düwel, *Das Opferfest von Lade,* 35 and 119–28.

86. As Erich Burger believes; see Burger, *Norwegische Stabkirchen: Geschichte— Bauweise—Schmuck* (Cologne: DuMont, 1978), 13–15.

87. Latin text in Boudriot, *Die altgermanische Religion,* 69.

88. On the general topic, see also the entry "Temples" in Simek, *Dictionary of Northern Mythology,* 310–12.

89. Tacitus, *Germania* (Tacitus, *The Agricola and the Germania*, 134). For original Latin with German trans., see Tacitus, *Germania* (1972), 16–17; Tacitus, *Germania* (1959), 24–25, and 82–85.

90. *Germania* (Tacitus, *The Agricola and the Germania*, 134). For original Latin with German trans., see Tacitus, *Germania* (1959), 53, 122–23.

91. Old English text (as far as it can be reconstructed) in Krapp and Dobbie, *The Anglo-Saxon Minor Poems*, 116–18; Karl Helm, *Altgermanische Religionsgeschichte*, vol. II, part 2: *Die Westgermanen* (Heidelberg: Winter, 1953), 235–36. Translation based on Müller, *Zeugnisse germanischer Religion*, 157, with elements from the version of Andreas Heusler.

Chapter 6. The Conception of the World (Cosmography)

1. See the entries in Simek, *Dictionary of Northern Mythology*, for "Midgard," 214, "Midgard serpent," 215, "Utgarðr", 343, "Jǫtunheim," 180, "Élivágar," 73, "Járnviðr," 179, "Yggdrasill," 375–76, "Irminsûl," 175–76, "Bifrǫst," 36–37, and "Asgard," 20.

2. Compare *Helgaviða Hundingsbana II* (Larrington, *The Poetic Edda*, 140, with the translation "bridge in the sky vault"). German: Niedner and Neckel, *Thule*, vol. 1, 160, with "Windhelms Brücke" (= Heavenly Bridge).

3. Compare "Muspilli" and the "Wessobrunn Prayer." The original Old High German texts can be found in Braune, *Althochdeutsches Lesebuch*. An English discussion of the poems (although lacking a full translation) appears in J. Knight Bostock, *A Handbook on Old High German Literature*, 2nd edition, revised by K. C. King and D. R. McLintock (Oxford: Oxford University Press, 1976), 126–4. Modern German translations appear in Friedrich von der Leyen, *Deutsches Mittelalter*, 1st edition (Frankfurt am Main: Insel-Verlag, 1980), 58–61.

4. Müller, *Zeugnisse germanischer Religion*, 108; Schröder, *Die Germanen*, 58–59. Translation by S. Alexandri.

5. Adam von Bremen, *Gesta Hammaburgensis ecclesiae pontificum* (Tschan, *The History of the Archbishops of Hamburg-Bremen*, 207–8). German: Schröder, *Die Germanen*, 61–62.

Chapter 7. The Beginnings of Time and the End Times

1. See *Vǫluspá* (Larrington, *The Poetic Edda*, 3–13), *Vǫluspá in skamma* (Bellows, *The Poetic Edda*, 217–33) and *Gylfaginning* (Sturluson, *Edda*, 9–14, 52–58). German: Schröder, *Die Germanen*, 48–53 and 53–54; *Thule*, vol. 20, 51–58, 110–16. On the relationship between Iranian and Germanic material, see Hans-Peter Hasenfratz, "Iran und der Dualismus," 44–46 and 51–52, and Hans-Peter Hasenfratz, "Iran:

Antagonismus als Universalprinzip," *Saeculum* 34 (1983), 244–47.

2. *Grímnismál, Vafþrúðnismál* (Larrington, *The Poetic Edda,* 57 and 43). German: Schröder, *Die Germanen,* 44 and 55.

3. *Germania* (Tacitus, *The Agricola and the Germania,* 102). For original Latin with German trans., see Tacitus, *Germania* (1959), 44 and 55.

4. Compare *Vafþrúðnismál* (Larrington, *The Poetic Edda,* 47). German: Schröder, *Die Germanen,* 56. Here and in the following notes, references will be given only for sources that are not contained in the texts cited in note 1, above.

5. Nordal, *Völuspá,* 91 and 93. German: Niedner and Neckel, *Thule,* vol. 2, 42, note to strophe 44. [The latter note by the editor of the text, Andreas Heusler, makes a claim that lines 1, 3, and 4 of strophe 44 were inspired by the biblical verse of Matthew 24:29. In the King James translation, this verse reads: "Immediately after the tribulation of those days shall the sun be darkened, and the moon shall not give her light, and the stars shall fall from heaven, and the powers of the heavens shall be shaken."—*Trans.*]

6. Compare *Vafþrúðnismál* (Larrington, *The Poetic Edda,* 47). German: Schröder, *Die Germanen,* 57.

7. Ström, "Germanische Religion," 248. According to written correspondence (dated 12/2/1991) from the runologist E. Ebel at Ruhr-Universität, Bochum, this reading of the inscription can still be upheld today. Compare *Vǫluspá* (Larrington, *The Poetic Edda,* 11 [end of strophe 52]). German: Niedner and Neckel, *Thule,* vol. 2, 41 (end of strophe 39).

8. *Heliand* (G. Ronald Murphy, S. J., trans., *The Heliand: The Saxon Gospel* [New York: Oxford University Press, 1992], 85 and 142). German: F. Genzmer, trans., *Heliand und die Bruchstücke der Genesis* (Stuttgart: Reclam, 1973), 89 and 138. Regarding "Muspilli," see Leyen, *Deutsches Mittelalter,* 60–61. On the interpretations of the word *muspilli* and a presentation of its documented forms, see Braune, *Althochdeutsches Lesebuch,* 170–71.

Bibliography

Amstadt, Jakob. *Südgermanische Religion seit der Völkerwanderungszeit.* Stuttgart: W. Kohlhammer, 1991.

Anderson, George K., trans. *The Saga of the Völsungs, Together with Excerpts from the Nornageststhátr and Three Chapters from the Prose Edda.* Newark: University of Delaware Press, 1982.

Bach, Adolf. *Geschichte der deutschen Sprache.* 6th edition. Heidelberg: Quelle and Meyer, 1956.

Bauchhenss, Gerhard, and Günter Neumann, eds. *Matronen und verwandte Gottheiten: Ergebnisse eines Kolloquiums veranstaltet von der Göttinger Akademiekommission für die Altertumskunde Mittel- und Nordeuropas.* Cologne and Bonn: Rheinland Verlag/Habelt, 1987.

Bechstein, Ludwig. *Der Sagenschatz des Frankenlandes, Erster Teil.* Würzburg: Voigt and Mocker, 1842.

Bellows, Henry Adams, trans. *The Poetic Edda.* New York: American-Scandinavian Foundation, 1923.

Bemmann, Klaus. *Der Glaube der Ahnen: Die Religion der Deutschen, bevor sie Christen wurden.* Essen: Phaidon, 1990.

Bostock, J. Knight. *A Handbook on Old High German Literature.* 2nd edition revised by K. C. King and D. R. McLintock. Oxford: Oxford University Press, 1976.

Boudriot, Wilhelm. *Die altgermanische Religion in der amtlichen kirchlichen Literatur des Abendlandes vom 5. bis 11. Jahrhundert.* Bonn: Ludwig Röhrscheid Verlag, 1964.

Braune, Wilhelm. *Althochdeutsches Lesebuch.* 14th edition. Tübingen: Niemeyer, 1964.

Breuer, Rolf, and Rainer Schöwerling, eds. *Altenglische Lyrik.* Stuttgart: Reclam, 1972.

Brunner, Heinrich. 1906. *Deutsche Rechtsgeschichte.* 2nd edition, 2 vols. Leipzig: Duncker and Humblot, 1906.

Burger, Erich. *Norwegische Stabkirchen: Geschichte—Bauweise—Schmuck.* Cologne: DuMont, 1978.

Byock, Jesse L., trans. *The Saga of the Volsungs: The Norse Epic of Sigurd the Dragon Slayer.* Berkeley: University of California Press, 1990.

———, trans. *The Saga of King Hrolf Kraki.* London: Penguin, 1998.

———, trans. *Grettir's Saga.* New York: Oxford University Press, 2009.

Chickering Jr., Howell D., trans. *Beowulf: A Dual-language Edition.* New York: Anchor, 2006.

The Complete Sagas of Icelanders. Edited by Viðar Hreinsson. Reykjavík: Leifur Eiríksson, 1997.

Cook, Robert, trans. *Njal's Saga.* London: Penguin, 2001.

Dennis, Andrew, Peter Foote, and Richard Perkins, trans. *Laws of Early Iceland: Grágás I.* Winnipeg: University of Manitoba Press, 1980.

Dumézil, Georges. *Loki.* Darmstadt: Wissenschaftliche Buchgesellschaft, 1959.

Düwel, Klaus, and Michael Gebühr. "Die Fibel von Meldorf und die Anfänge der Runenschrift." *Zeitschrift für Deutsches Altertum und deutsche Literatur* 110 (1981): 159–77.

Düwel, Klaus. "Das Opferfest von Lade: Quellenkritische Untersuchungen zur germanischen Religionsgeschichte," *Wiener Arbeiten zur germanischen Altertumskunde und Philologie* 27. Vienna: Halosar, 1985.

———. "Buchstabenmagie und Alphabetzauber: Zu den Inschriften der Goldbrakteaten und ihrer Function als Amulette." *Früh Mittelalterliche Studien* 22 (1988): 70–110.

Ellwood, Rev. T., trans. *The Book of the Settlement of Iceland, Translated from the Original Icelandic of Ari the Learned.* Kendal: T. Wilson, 1898.

Ettmüller, Ludwig. *Altnordischer Sagenschatz in neun Büchern.* Leipzig: Verlag von Friedrich Fleischer, 1870.

Faulkes, Anthony, ed. *Stories from the Sagas of the Kings.* London: Viking Society for Northern Research, 1980.

Ferdowsi. *The Epic of the Kings.* Translated by Reuben Levy. London: Routledge and Kegan Paul, 1967.

Fest, Joachim C. *Hitler.* Translated by Richard and Clara Winston. New York: Harcourt Brace Jovanovich, 1974.

Genzmer, F., trans. *Heliand und die Bruchstücke der Genesis.* Stuttgart: Reclam, 1973.

———, trans. *Beowulf und das Finnsburg-Bruchstück.* Stuttgart: Reclam, 1975.

Gitermann, Valentin. *Die Geschichte Russlands,* vol. 1. Zurich: Büchergilde Gutenberg, 1944.

Golther, Wolfgang. *Handbuch der germanischen Mythologie.* Reprint of 2nd edition [1908]. Kettwig: Magnus-Verlag, 1985.

Graf, Heinz-Joachim. *Orientalische Berichte des Mittelalters über die Germanen: Eine Quellensammlung.* Krefeld: Verlag Schnelldruck F. Thyssen, 1971.

Grimm, Jacob. *Teutonic Mythology.* Reprint of 4th edition, 1883–1886. 4 vols. Translated by James Steven Stallybrass. Gloucester, Mass.: Peter Smith, 1976.

———. *Deutsche Rechtsalterthümer.* Reprint of 4th edition. 2 vols. Darmstadt: Wissenschaftliche Buchgesellschaft, 1983.

Grønlie, Siân. *Íslendingabók, Kristni saga: The Book of the Icelanders, The Story of the Conversion.* London: Viking Society for Northern Research, 2006.

Grönbech, Vilhelm. *The Culture of the Teutons.* 3 vols. London: Oxford University Press, 1932.

Gschwantler, Otto, and Knut Schäferdiek. "Bekehrung und Bekehrungsgeschichte." In *Reallexikon der Germanischen Altertumskunde,* 2nd edition. Berlin: Walter De Gruyter, 1976.

Gutenbrunner, Siegfried. *Historische Laut- und Formenlehre des Altisländischen; zugleich eine Einführung in das Urnordische.* Heidelberg: Winter, 1951.

Haller, Johannes, and Heinrich Dannenbauer. *Der Eintritt der Germanen in die Geschichte.* 4th edition. Berlin: Walter De Gruyter, 1970.

Hasenfratz, Hans-Peter. *Die toten Lebenden: Eine religionsphänomenologische Studie zum sozialen Tod in archaischen Gesellschaften, zugleich ein kritischer Beitrag zur sogenannten Strafopfertheorie.* Beihefte zur Zeitschrift für Religions- und Geistesgeschichte 24. Leiden: Brill, 1982.

———. "Der indogermanische 'Männerbund': Anmerkungen zur religiösen und sozialen Bedeutung des Jugendalters." *Zeitschrift für Religions- und Geistesgeschichte* 34, no. 2 (1982): 148–63.

———. "Iran und der Dualismus." *Numen* 30, no. 30, fasc.1 (July 1983): 35–52.

———. "Iran: Antagonismus als Universalprinzip." *Saeculum* 34 (1983): 235–47.

———. "Seelenvorstellungen bei den Germanen und ihre Übernahme und Umformung durch die christliche Mission." *Zeitschrift für Religions- und Geistesgeschichte* 38, no. 1 (1986): 19–31.

———. *Die Seele: Einführung in ein religiöses Grundphänomen.* Zürich: Theologischer Verlag, 1986.

———. "Germanische Religion." In Franz König and Heinz Waldenfels, eds. *Lexikon der Religionen.* Freiburg: Herder, 1987.

———. "Die Religion Alfred Rosenbergs," *Numen* 36, fasc. 1 (June 1989): 113–26.

———. "Krieg und Frieden bei den alten Germanen." In Gerhard Binder and Bernd Effe, eds. *Krieg und Frieden im Altertum.* Trier: Wissenschaftlicher Verlag, 1989.

Heiduczek, Werner and Dorothea. *Die schönsten Sagen aus Firdausis Königsbuch.* Hanau: Kinderbuch Verlag, 1982.

Helm, Karl. *Altgermanische Religionsgeschichte,* vol. 2, part 2: *Die Westgermanen.* Heidelberg: Winter, 1953.

Hermann, Paul. *Das altgermanische Priesterwesen.* Jena: Diederichs, 1929.

Hollander, Lee M., trans. *The Saga of the Jómsvíkings.* Austin: University of Texas Press, 1990.

———, trans. *Old Norse Poems: The Most Important Non-Skaldic Verse Not Included in the Poetic Edda.* New York: Columbia University Press, 1936.

Hunke, Sigrid. *Europas eigene Religion.* Bergisch-Gladbach: Bastei Lubbe, 1983.

Jacob, Georg. *Iskenders Warägerfeldzug: Ein iranischer Heldensang des Mittelalters aus Nizâmî's Iskendernâme.* Glückstadt: J. J. Augustin, 1934.

Jantzen, H., trans. *Saxo Grammaticus: Die ersten neun Bücher der dänischen Geschichte.* Berlin: Verlag von Emil Felber, 1900.

Kilian, Lothar. *Zum Ursprung der Germanen.* Bonn: Habelt, 1988.

König, Franz and Heinz Waldenfels, eds. *Lexikon der Religionen.* Freiburg: Herder, 1987.

Krapp, George P. and Elliott Van Kirk Dobbie, eds. *The Exeter Book.* New York: Columbia University Press, 1936.

———, eds. *The Anglo-Saxon Minor Poems.* New York: Columbia University Press, 1942.

Krüger, Bruno, ed. *Die Germanen: Geschichte und Kultur der germanischen Stämme in Mitteleuropa.* 2 vols. Darmstadt: Wissenschaftliche Buchgesellschaft, 1987–88.

Larrington, Carolyn, trans. *The Poetic Edda.* Oxford: Oxford University Press, 1996.

Leyen, Friedrich von der. *Deutsches Mittelalter.* 1st edition. Frankfurt: Insel-Verlag, 1980.

Larson, Laurence M., trans. *The Earliest Norwegian Laws: Being the Gulathing Law and the Frostathing Law.* New York: Columbia University Press, 1935.

Marzell, Heinrich. "Bilsenkraut." In *Handwörterbuch des Deutschen Aberglaubens.* Reprint of 1st edition. Berlin and New York: Walter De Gruyter, 1987.

McKinnell, John, trans. *Viga-Glums Saga, with the Tales of Ögmund Bash and Thorvald Chatterbox.* Edinburgh: Canongate/UNESCO, 1987.

Meissner, Rudolph, ed. and trans. *Norwegisches Recht: Das Rechtsbuch des Gulathings.* Weimar: Böhlau, 1935.

Müller, Georg. *Zeugnisse germanischer Religion, Kirche und Erziehung.* Pädogogische Schriftenreihe der evangelischen Schulverein 9 (1935).

Murphy, G. Ronald, S. J., trans. *The Heliand: The Saxon Gospel.* New York: Oxford University Press, 1992.

Naumann, Hans and Ida, trans. *Isländische Volksmärchen.* Jena: Diederichs, 1923.

Niedner, F. and Gustav Neckel, eds. *Thule: Altnordische Dichtung und Prosa.* 24

vols. Reprint of 1912–1930 edition. Düsseldorf and Cologne: Wissenschaftliche Buchgesellschaft, 1963–1967.

Nordal, Sigurður, ed. *Völuspá. Aus dem Isländischen übersetzt und mit einem Vorwort zur deutschen Ausgabe von Ommo Wilts.* Darmstadt: Wissenschaftliche Buchgesellschaft, 1980.

Pálsson, Hermann, and Paul Edwards, trans. *Gautrek's Saga and Other Medieval Tales.* London: University of London Press, 1968.

———, trans. *The Book of Settlements: Landnámabók.* Winnipeg: University of Manitoba Press, 1972.

———, trans. *Orkneyinga saga: The History of the Earls of Orkney.* London: Hogarth, 1978.

Quirk, Randolph and C. L. Wrenn. *An Old English Grammar.* 2nd edition. London: Methuen, 1960.

The Sagas of Icelanders. New York: Viking, 2001.

Saxo Grammaticus. *The History of the Danes, Books I–IX.* Edited and translated by Hilda Ellis Davidson and Peter Fisher. Woodbridge: Brewer, 1996.

Schach, Paul, and Lee M. Hollander, trans. *Eyrbyggja Saga.* Lincoln: University of Nebraska Press, 1959.

Schier, Kurt, ed. and trans. *Die Saga von Egil.* Darmstadt: Wissenschaftliche Buchgesellschaft, 1978.

Schreiber, Hermann. *Die Zehn Gebote: Der Mensch und sein Recht.* 1st edition. Vienna and Düsseldorf: Econ-Verlag, 1962.

Schröder, Franz Rolf. *Die Germanen.* Tübingen: Mohr, 1929.

Seelow, Hubert, ed. and trans. *Die Saga von Grettir.* 1st edition. Darmstadt: Wissenschaftliche Buchgesellschaft, 1974.

Simek, Rudolf, and Hermann Pálsson. *Lexikon der altnordischen Literatur.* Stuttgart: Kröner, 1987.

Simek, Rudolf. *Dictionary of Northern Mythology.* Cambridge: D. S. Brewer, 1993.

Simpson, Jacqueline. *Icelandic Folktales and Legends.* Berkeley: University of California Press, 1972.

Smyser, H. M. "Ibn Faḍlān's Account of the Rūs, with Some Commentary and Some Allusions to *Beowulf.*" In Jess B. Bessinger and Robert P. Creed, eds. *Franciplegius: Medieval and Linguistic Studies in Honor of Francis Peabody Magoun, Jr.* New York: New York University Press, 1965.

Snorrason, Oddr. *The Saga of Olaf Tryggvason.* Translated by Theodore M. Andersson. Ithaca: Cornell University Press, 2003.

Steller, Walther. "Pferdekopf." In *Handwörterbuch des deutschen Aberglaubens,* vol. 6. Berlin and New York: Walter De Gruyter, 1987.

Strauch, Dieter, trans. *Das Ostgötenrecht (Östgötalagen)*. Cologne: Böhlau Verlag, 1971.

Ström, Åke V. "Germanische Religion." In *Die Religionen der Menschheit,* vol. 19, part 1. Stuttgart: Kohlhammer, 1975.

Ström, Folke. *On the Sacral Origin of the Germanic Death Penalties.* Lund: Håkan Ohlssons Boktryckeri, 1942.

Streitberg, Wilhelm. *Die Gotische Bibel.* Heidelberg: Winter, 1971.

Sturluson, Snorri. *Heimskringla: History of the Kings of Norway.* Translated by Lee M. Hollander. Austin: University of Texas Press, 1964.

———. *Edda.* Translated by Anthony Faulkes. London: Dent, 1987.

Tacitus, Publius Cornelius. *Germania.* Edited and translated by Eugen Fehrle and Richard Hünnerkopf. 5th edition. Heidelberg: Winter, 1959.

Tacitus, Cornelius. *The Agricola and the Germania.* Translated by H. Mattingly. London: Penguin, 1970.

Tacitus. *Germania.* Edited and translated by Manfred Fuhrmann. Stuttgart: Reclam, 1972.

Terry, Patricia, trans. *Poems of the Elder Edda.* Revised edition. Philadelphia: University of Pennsylvania Press, 1990.

Thorpe, Benjamin. 2001. *Northern Mythology: From Pagan Faith to Local Legends.* Ware, Hertfordshire: Wordsworth Editions, 2001.

Togan, Ahmed Zeki Validi. *Ibn Faḍlān's Reisebericht.* Leipzig: Deutsche Morgenländische Gesellschaft, 1939.

Tschan, Francis J., trans. *The History of the Archbishops of Hamburg-Bremen by Adam of Bremen.* New York: Columbia University Press, 2002.

Völger, Gisela and Karin von Welck, eds. *Männerbünde–Männerbande: Zur Rolle des Mannes im Kulturvergleich.* 2 vols. Cologne: Rautenstrauch-Joest-Museum, 1990.

Vordemfelde, Hans. *Die germanische Religion in den deutschen Volksrechten; Erster Halbband: Der religiöse Glaube.* Religionsgeschichtliche Versuche und Vorarbeiten 18:1. Giessen: Verlag von Alfred Töpelmann, 1923.

Vries, Jan de. *Altgermanische Religionsgeschichte.* 3rd edition, 2 vols. Berlin: Walter De Gruyter, 1970.

———. *Altnordisches etymologisches Wörterbuch.* 2nd edition. Leiden: Brill, 1977.

Widengren, Geo, ed. *Iranische Geisteswelt: Von den Anfängen bis zum Islam.* Baden-Baden: Holle, 1961.

Index